THE DREAM AND THE GRACE

THE DREAM
AND THE GRACE

SERMONS ON HEALTHY
AND UNHEALTHY RELIGION

JAMES A. WHYTE

SAINT ANDREW PRESS
EDINBURGH

For Ishbel

First published in 2001 by
SAINT ANDREW PRESS
121 George Street
Edinburgh
EH2 4YN

ISBN 0 7152 0777 6

British Library Cataloguing in Publication Data
A catalogue record for this book is available from the British Library.

Cover design by McColl Productions, Edinburgh

Typeset in Dutch 801 by Hugh K. Clarkson & Sons Ltd, Young Street, West Calder, West Lothian EH55 8EG

Printed and bound in the United Kingdom by
Bell & Bain Ltd., Glasgow

CONTENTS

Introduction   1

1. The Dream of the Perfect Round
   (Annual Service for Golfers, St Andrews,
   Holy Trinity, 14 September 1997)   3
2. Ideals – Who Needs Them?   9
3. All Change   15
4. The Far-Seeing Eye
   (West Kirk of Helensburgh, 14 August 1988,
   to mark the centenary of the birth of
   John Logie Baird)   21
5. The Microchip and the Paper Clip   27
6. Fanaticism and Faith   34
7. The Fortress and the Fog
   (University of St Andrews, Commemoration of
   Founders and Benefactors, 27 February 2000)   40
8. Religious or Superstitious?   46
9. Standing on the Shoulders of Giants   52
10. The Work of God   58
11. Unity and Tolerance
    (First preached during the Week of Prayer for
    Christian Unity, 19 January 1961)   64
12. Unity and Love
    (Preached at the centenary of St Stephen's
    Church, Inverness, 19 October 1997)   71
13. Getting off the Ground
    (Service of Inauguration of the Scottish
    Congregational Church, 19 September 1993)   77
14. Excluding and Including   83
15. Age and Youth Together
    (Presentation of long-service certificate,
    Carnbee, 6 July 1997)   90
16. The Tourist and the Exile
    (Opening service of the American Summer
    Institute, St Andrews, 27 June 1976)   96

17. Peace on the Train   102
18. Health Abundant
     (Service for the 50th anniversary of the
     National Health Service, St Mary's,
     Dundee, 5 July 1998)   108
19. Curing or Coping?   114
20. The Reign of Christ the King   120
21. Out of Darkness into Light
     (Memorial Service for the 16 children and
     their teacher who were killed in Dunblane
     Primary School, 13 March 1996. Held in
     Dunblane Cathedral, 9 October 1996)   125

INTRODUCTION

WHEN I was in my first charge my father kept buying me volumes of Spurgeon's sermons, which he bought at Henderson's second-hand department on George IV Bridge, Edinburgh. He was a businessman, not a theologian, but he thought this would encourage me in my task. I appreciated his kindness, but not, at first, the gift, because I was convinced then, and am even more convinced now, that no one may preach someone else's sermon. A sermon is a personal utterance. Prayers are different. They are intended to be corporate utterances. Sermons are where we speak to our people, as honestly as we can, what we believe God has to say to them. Therefore we are at liberty to use other people's prayers, but not their sermons. So Spurgeon's *Metropolitan Tabernacle Pulpit* sat on the shelves, unused. What had a nineteenth-century Baptist preacher to say to me, a mid-twentieth-century Presbyterian? Then one day it happened, as it comes to all preachers, that I was dry and could get nothing from the lectionary or from my own casting around. I took Spurgeon from the shelf and began to read one of his sermons. It was much more interesting than I had expected, and full of humour. It stimulated my tired mind, and I found myself arguing with him and disagreeing with his treatment of the text. The book was closed, the commentaries came out, and I began writing my own sermon on Spurgeon's text, a sermon which was quite different from his.

If a preacher does that with mine I shall not be disappointed, but sermons are not preached or published for the sake of preachers, but for people, who may, one hopes, find something in them that lights up their experience or opens their hearts to faith. Those in this collection have been preached in various places, and some of them more than once in different forms. They range in time from a sermon on unity, which was first preached in 1961, and shows, to my surprise, how early my views on church unity were formed, to the latest sermon which I have written. The collection begins with a sermon for the Annual Golfers' Service in St Andrews, and ends with the sermon preached at the Memorial Service for the children and their teacher who were massacred at Dunblane on 13 March 1996. So there are different moods, but I hope that some themes run through, which might even reveal a consistent theology of grace.

The quotation on pp. 3–4 from John Updike's novel *Rabbit at Rest* (New York: Fawcett Crest, 1991, p. 45) is printed by kind permission of the author and of the publisher, Alfred A. Knopf, a Division of Random House Inc. The quotation on pp. 40–1 from *A History Book for Scots: Selections from* Scotichronicon, by Walter Bower, edited by D. E. R. Watt (Edinburgh: Mercat Press, 1998, pp. 263–4), is printed by kind permission of the University of St Andrews. Biblical quotations are from the RSV.

I am grateful to those who asked me to preach, and to the congregations who listened. And I am forever grateful for the encouragement I used to receive from Elisabeth, and now get, with much kindness, from Ishbel.

James Aitken Whyte
St Andrews

1 THE DREAM OF THE PERFECT ROUND

*Annual Service for Golfers, St Andrews, Holy Trinity,
14 September 1997*

Readings: Genesis 11:1–9; II Corinthians 12:1–10

Text: II Corinthians 12:9 *But he said to me, My grace is
sufficient for you, for my power is made perfect in weakness.*

JOHN Updike, the American novelist, seems to have got
hooked on golf, and has actually written a book about it.
I haven't read that, but in one novel of his, which I
recently read, the principal character is on the first tee of his
golf course in Florida, and this is what he thinks as he
prepares to drive off.

> Always, golf for him holds out the hope of perfection,
> of a perfect weightlessness and consummate ease, for
> now and again it does happen, happens in three
> dimensions, shot after shot. But then he gets human
> and tries to force it, to make it happen, to get ten extra
> yards, to steer it, and it goes away, grace you would call
> it, the feeling of collaboration, of being bigger than he
> really is. When you stand up on the first tee it is there,
> it comes back from wherever it lives during the rest of
> your life, endless possibility, the possibility of a
> flawless round, a round without a speck of dirt in it,
> without a missed two-footer or a flying right elbow,
> without a pushed wood or a pulled iron; the first
> fairway is in front of you, palm-trees on the left and
> water on the right, flat as a picture. All you have to do
> is take a simple pure swing and puncture the picture in
> the middle with a ball that shrinks in a second to the

3

size of a needle-prick, a tiny tunnel into the absolute. That would be *it*.

But of course it isn't. Harry's drive goes into the water.

I speak to you as one who gave up golf many years ago. Perhaps it would be truer to say that golf gave me up, for I never was any good at it. But I can understand the feelings of Harry Angstrom as he stands on the first tee of his course in Florida. Each time you stand on that tee you have before you what I would call the dream of the perfect round, when the ball will go straight down the middle of the fairway, and the approach shot will be pin-high, and the putt will go down. Somehow, in spite of all our sad experience of the rounds we have actually played, we still have that dream.

But in John Updike's description of Harry's feeling on the first tee I find a theological word, a religious word, in a strange setting. It's the word 'grace'. Grace, you would call it, the feeling of collaboration, of being bigger than you really are. Then, sometimes, strangely, things go right. You hit it straight down the middle, and for a few strokes, even a hole or two, the game seems simple, effortless enjoyment.

But it doesn't last. You get human. You try to force it, and soon you are renewing your acquaintance with the whins and the thick rough, and the bunkers seem to have been positioned specially for you, and you tense up, and your game goes to pieces. The next time you stand on the first tee, the dream returns. The dream of the perfect round. And that dream, perpetually returning, yet perpetually disappointed, seems like a parable of human life. High hopes and sad experiences. Trying so hard – too hard, perhaps – to get it right, and then not getting it right at all.

The Old Testament story we read is another parable of human life. It is a very old and very odd story. We don't know who these people are. They seem to represent the whole human race. They come into the great Mesopotamian plain, and they feel very insecure and afraid. So they decide to build a tower so high it will reach to heaven. Then they will

4

be like gods, moving between heaven and earth. Then it will be OK.

They want to get it right, by making themselves bigger than they really are. And it goes dreadfully wrong. God confounds their language, the building is never finished, and they are scattered over the face of the earth. Their game has gone to pieces.

This is no doubt the attempt of an ancient storyteller to explain why different tribes and nations speak different languages. They all spoke the same tongue once, he says, but it went to bits. And he linked that with an explanation of the towers, the ziggurats, which were once to be found on the great plain of Babylon. Like many an old story it's not scientifically or historically true, but it contains a truth about human life. Specifically, about why things go wrong.

For things have gone and do go wrong. We have a dream of how things ought to be, but, like the dream of the perfect round, it is soon shattered. People don't understand one another, even when they're speaking the same language. We build our towers – political policies, institutions, churches – and sometimes we think we've got it right, but it doesn't last, and often not for very long. Even in the most loving families, there is misunderstanding, and conflict, and pain. Why?

Why? The old storyteller suggests that the people in his story were anxious and insecure, afraid of being scattered over the earth. They tried to avoid that by building this tower of pride, to make themselves big, like gods who could reach to heaven. When we do that, he says, God himself takes a hand, and the whole thing goes to pieces. The very thing they most dreaded happens to them, and they are scattered over the face of the earth.

John Updike's analysis of the game of golf is remarkably similar. He starts with the dream, the dream of the perfect round, the possibility that it can be different this time. And sometimes, sometimes it is for a little time. Everything gels and it goes right, and easily and without undue effort the ball flies in the right direction. And, surprisingly, Updike calls that 'grace'. 'Grace you might call it,' he says. Why does it not last? Because we try to force it. We get human. We become anxious and tense. We try to get that extra ten yards. We push it. And it goes to pieces and we are all over the place. Our anxiety and our self-concern banish the gentle experience of grace.

I am not suggesting, nor would John Updike, that you will all become scratch golfers if you attend a service like this and pray humbly for grace before you mount the first tee. Or that God favours the pious rather than the sceptic on the fairway or around the greens. My own sad experience suggests that that is not so.

If I may say so in this company, I am inclined to think that God does not take golf as seriously as some golfers do. He looks indulgently on it, no doubt, but there are many other things going on in his universe. So if God has not yet made you the perfect golfer, don't think too hardly of him for that. Maybe he has other, and more important things for you to do. Yet Updike seems to suggest that if you weren't trying so anxiously to make yourself the perfect golfer, your handicap might actually come down. Is that true? I leave it to you. I'm not qualified to judge, for I gave the game up years ago, and now walk the Old Course on a Sunday afternoon.

I could give up golf, because it is only a game. But I cannot give up living. No use saying, 'I'm no good at living, I'll opt out.' But in my living the dream and the reality, the high hopes and the sad experiences, are too often very far apart. If I dream of myself as a superior person, there are an awful lot of things waiting to shatter that dream.

Look now at the experience of Paul. He had had some very special and intense spiritual experiences. God had turned his life around, opened his eyes to the truth, and called him to preach and to show to others the depths of God's love and forgiveness, the riches of his grace in Jesus Christ. He had had a mystical experience which he calls being in the third heaven. But at the same time he had a chronic illness, a complaint which kept getting in the way and hindering his progress. We don't know what it was. It may have been a form of epilepsy. It was certainly embarrassing. He called it a thorn in the flesh, a messenger of Satan to buffet him.

Not only was this a painful nuisance to him personally, but it made other people look down on him, strange little fellow that he was. His work was hindered. But Paul had a dream. The dream of the superior person – in his case, the dream of the perfect preacher. How much better it would be if he were rid of this weakness, if he were, and were seen to be, a powerful, perfectly healthy man! Then folks would be impressed, and they would pay attention to what he was saying. God had done so much for him, surely he would do this too, a small miracle, to equip Paul better for God's service.

So Paul prayed. And he prayed. And he prayed again. And nothing happened. So he stopped praying and started to think. It might have been better if he had thought first and prayed afterwards. That's often the way. Anyway, when Paul did start to think he realised that God was saying, 'No. You have to put up with this. You must learn to live with your weakness, and rely not on your own strength or skill, but on mine. My grace is enough for you. My power is made perfect in weakness.'

Now that's grace. But is it the same or different from what Updike was talking about? Updike was thinking of that effortless ease which sometimes comes to us, that makes us feel bigger than we are. That is the dream realised – even if only for a moment. What Paul experienced was the grace that comes when the dream has departed. He has to give up the dream of being a superior person, always on top of things, never struggling, never cast down. He can only be his own size, not perfect, but sadly aware of his own inadequacies and disabilities.

Then the true miracle began. Not the one he had prayed for and dreamed of, but something better. He doesn't have to build a tower up to heaven, to make himself feel bigger than he is. Heaven reaches down to him, takes his disability and turns it to advantage, takes his inadequacy and makes it sufficient, and covers all his mistakes with loving forgiveness.

The dreams are all right, in a way. They point us in the right direction. But when we realise that we can't turn that dream into reality, no matter how hard we try, it is good if we too can hear one who says, 'My grace is sufficient for you, for my power is made perfect in weakness.'

Let us pray.

Dear Master, in whose life I see
All that I would but fail to be,
Let Thy clear light for ever shine,
To shame and guide this life of mine.

Though what I dream and what I do
In my weak days are always two,
Help me, oppressed by things undone,
O Thou, whose deeds and dreams were one!

2 IDEALS – WHO NEEDS THEM?

Readings: Leviticus 19:11–18; Matthew 5:21–24, 38–48

Text: Matthew 5:48 *You, therefore, must be perfect, as your heavenly Father is perfect.*

'IDEALS – who needs them?' The question was asked in a book I read recently.

'Ideals – who needs them?' My first response was indignant. We all need ideals. We need something to aim at, something to pull us forward. Without ideals we lack direction. Without ideals we all become cynics who know the price of everything and the value of nothing. It sometimes seems this world is being run and overrun by multinational corporations whose only value is the fast buck, with no care about the consequences for the environment or for the poor. The employment practices of many of the big businesses and banks suggest that to them money, the bottom line, is everything and people matter not at all.

And don't we need ideals in public life? I think I'm not the only one to be disappointed at the level of political debate in Scotland today. We had hoped for a more open and honest politics in a devolved Scotland. People in Britain and the United States have lost faith in politicians because politics seems to be a dirty game, where principles can be abandoned for power or profit, and where you aim to win by fair means or foul. One ex-minister said that governments have no obligation to tell the truth, either to Parliament or to the public. That sees power, gained and held by any means, as the only goal of politics. And that in turn leads to corruption, to sleaze. Do we not need ideals of truth and honour to make politics credible again?

That was my first thought. Then I thought again. Ideals can be unrealistic, harsh, unforgiving and uncompromising. An ideal is a standard of perfection. An idealist may be so in love with his idea of a perfect society that he is intolerant of anything less. The idealist is a revolutionary who wishes to destroy the present in order to build the perfect future. The reformer takes what we've got and tries to make it a bit better. The reformer usually does more good than the revolutionary. The perfect society of the idealist never comes, or is far from perfect, as communist tyrannies have shown. Maybe what our politicians need is not ideals, but rather vision – the attainable vision of a better society.

All of us make do with what is imperfect. We do that in our personal lives as well as in our politics. However happy our marriages – and I hope they are – we none of us married the perfect wife or the perfect husband: nor did our spouses. We all have faults, hang-ups, problems. We are imperfect human beings. No one sings the perfect song, preaches the perfect sermon, teaches the perfect lesson, cooks the perfect meal or whatever. Our achievements are all flawed. They may be quite good, very good, indeed, but not perfect. Those who think so deceive themselves, like the young man who announced, 'I used to be conceited. But now, I'm perfect.'

That is no reason for being like the other young man, who was on the carpet before the boss, and told roundly that he was no good, lazy, unpunctual, dishonest, rude, stupid and incompetent. He replied with a shrug, 'Well, no one's perfect.' True no one is perfect, but that is no excuse for being complacent. We could be better. We need vision – realistic vision.

Then I thought again. There are false ideals, which can be very hurtful. Some people – many, perhaps – think they are unattractive because they don't fit some ideal of beauty – an ideal created by magazines, and advertisements, beauticians and hairdressers. 'There is no such thing as natural beauty', says Truvy the hairdresser in the play *Steel Magnolias*. By that she means that no one is beautiful until they have been tarted up by her. How wrong she was. The other day I saw a bit of a TV programme where an elderly lady was remembering her first day working in an office. The girl who was assigned to help her went on later to be a star. The show brought them, both now in their seventies, together for the first time since then. The contrast between the sweet natural lady and the glamorous, platinum-blonde star was striking, and I had no doubt which was more beautiful. In fact, few great actresses in the theatre have the beauty of a photographic model. Some are rather plain. But when the character they are playing shines through them, they become beautiful, transfigured by the life within. Love and laughter, and sometimes the dignity of tears, can make ordinary people radiate beauty. But false ideals of beauty – which change, of course, with changing fashion – can cause much unhappiness and discouragement.

Religion can produce false ideals: a false ideal of holiness or a false ideal of chastity, for example. When I was a boy I was briefly involved in what was then called the Oxford Group, with its Four Absolutes – Absolute Honesty, Absolute Purity, Absolute Unselfishness and Absolute Love. I won't say anything about the others, but the one which gave adolescents most trouble and got most attention was Absolute Purity. It was some time after I left the Oxford Group that I saw that behind this lay a false and unhealthy view of sex. The natural curiosity of the young, which society is afraid to satisfy, was condemned as 'dirty thoughts', and God's good gift of sex, instead of being happily directed towards lasting love and joy, was sullied as unclean. We were made to feel guilty for being human. A wise man once said, 'To the pure, all things are dirty.'

The Oxford Group is not entirely to blame for this, because the unhealthy view of sex goes back to the early centuries, to Tertullian and to Augustine, and colours the whole history of the church. It has caused, and causes still, much unnecessary unhappiness and unnecessary guilt. The Roman Catholic Church still regards marriage as second-best to celibacy.

Ideals, true or false, may lead to guilt and to despair, or else to self-deception. People who believe they really are pure, or unselfish, may keep the unacceptable side of themselves carefully hidden, except when it comes out in condemnation of other people. Idealists can be very censorious. When I hear an Archbishop call life-long monogamous marriage 'an ideal', I know he's about to condemn anything else. But life-long monogamous marriage may be hell for some people, no ideal.

Now let us look at our text. Matthew 5:48: 'You, therefore, must be perfect, as your heavenly Father is perfect.' Surely this is an ideal. By definition an ideal is a standard of perfection. Surely there can be no higher ideal than this. 'Be perfect, as your heavenly Father is perfect.'

Does this ideal encourage us, or does it lead us to guilt and to despair, or tempt us into self-deception?

Look again at the verses we read from the Sermon on the Mount.

> You have heard that it was said to the men of old, 'You shall not kill; and whoever kills shall be liable to judgment.' But I say to you that everyone who is angry with his brother shall be liable to judgment, whoever insults his brother shall be liable to the council, and whoever says, 'You fool', shall be liable to the hell of fire.

Here, anger, insult and contempt are seen as just as serious as murder. Indeed, contempt, despising your brother, seems the most serious sin of all. So what do we do about that, you and me? Do we go for self-deception? Do we pretend that we are always calm, never angry, never looking down on the poor mutt who got things wrong?

What do you do with your anger? Don't tell me you are

never angry, for I won't believe you. A while ago, I got very angry indeed with the Gas Board. It was a long saga of dangerous incompetence, and then of many frustrating phone calls and visits to our house while the buck was passed from one company, one department, one sub-contractor to another, till I was climbing the wall. Finally one sub-contractor who was not responsible for the mess took pity on me and came and put things right. To crown it all, I got a bill from the Gas Board for the work which might well have killed us.

I was angry, very, very angry. My anger was, I think, justified. I wasn't angry at individuals, such as the girls called Kylie or Terry who couldn't help but gave me yet another number to phone. I wasn't even angry at the workman whose carelessness left us in danger, for he was clearly under great pressure to complete so many calls in a day. I was angry at a system that was frustrating them and me, and at the faceless, senseless managers who devised it. What to do with my anger?

The first thing was to go to the bottlebank for a therapeutic smash. The second was to sit down and compose a long and detailed letter of complaint. My anger subsided. When we get angry, as all of us do, we have to find some creative and positive way of dealing with our anger, so that it leads to helpful, rather than destructive, action. Jesus, it seems, dealt so with his own anger, against the Pharisees and on behalf of the sick and the poor.

What of the Sermon on the Mount, which speaks of not resisting evil, turning the other cheek, loving your enemies? When I was young I took that to be an ideal of non-violence, and I was a pacifist. During the war I came to see that you do not best love your enemies by allowing them to trample over your friends in hobnailed boots. Yet I still believe that to love and not to hate remains the call of Jesus. Hatred and resentment are always destructive forces that separate us from ourselves, from others, and from God.

All the difficult demands of the Sermon on the Mount are summed up in the call 'Be perfect, as your heavenly Father is perfect.' This must be the highest, most rigorous, most unforgiving ideal. 'Be perfect.' Must it not lead us to guilt, or to despair, or to self-deception, because however hard we try we are not perfect?

But is this an ideal at all? Ideals are cold, impersonal abstractions. They give us direction and something to aim at, but they are harsh and unforgiving when we fall short – and they make us harsh and unforgiving to others when they fall short. Jesus is not offering us an ideal. He is offering us a heavenly Father. 'Be perfect, as your heavenly Father is perfect.' God's perfection is not a cold ideal, it is his grace, his love of his enemies – that is, of you and me and all selfish, sinning humanity. God's perfection is his forgiveness, his reconciling love. Go back and read the Sermon on the Mount with that in mind, and you will find it is not a harsh and unforgiving ideal, but an invitation to life, in the warmth of his forgiving love.

Ideals, who needs them? Perhaps only those who have not yet discovered the warmth of the heavenly Father's transforming and forgiving love, the grace that can make all things new.

May that grace keep transforming us.

14

3 ALL CHANGE

Readings: 2 Samuel 22:1–20, 26–31; II Corinthians 3:17–4:7

Text: II Corinthians 3:18 *And we all, with unveiled face, beholding the glory of the Lord, are being changed into his likeness, from one degree of glory to another; for this comes from the Lord who is the Spirit.*

'ALL change,' said the tram-conductor, passing through the top deck of the tram. 'All change.'

We protested. 'We're going to Goldenacre and this is only Canonmills.'

'We're turning here,' he said. 'You can get the next tram to Goldenacre.'

So we got off, grumbling and complaining.

That sort of thing used to happen on Edinburgh trams. 'All change!' And you had to get off.

Some people are crying, 'All change,' in the church today. They're not asking us to get off. They even think others might get on. 'Change' has become a battle-cry of the progressive, almost a party slogan. Like those in Corinth who cried, 'I'm for Paul,' or, 'Apollos is the boy for me,' or, 'I stick with Peter,' we have those who cry, 'I'm for change.'

I hear preachers saying things must change; I read articles calling for change; I hear ministers at inductions telling congregations that they must be ready for change; I have even heard ex-moderators singing the praises of change. You might say it has become quite a fashion. Almost a new gospel. And that makes me suspicious.

For not all change is change for the better. Change may be good for you or bad for you. We need to discriminate. Some changes are changes for the worse. Those who are zealous to throw out the dirty bathwater may not have noticed there was a baby in the tub as well. Change for the sake of change does nothing.

My dear sister-in-law was always restless. Although she was quite good at making friends with her neighbours, she was always attracted by somewhere else. She and her patient husband kept moving house. And while the new gave some excitement for a little time, it soon palled. The changes of scene that she made did not touch the fundamental dissatisfaction in her life. It is no use changing outward things if your deeper problems remain untouched.

Something like that seems to go on in the church. All the boards and committees of the church have been reorganised in the past few years, and I don't know what any of them is called now. But has anything really changed? Salvation by reorganisation is well known in business, in the universities and in the health service too today, where it is known as 'Management'. When managers don't know what to do, and feel the need to justify their existence, they reorganise their sections, faculties, boards, committees, or what-have-you, call them by different names and then sit back with the comfortable feeling that something has been accomplished. In fact, nothing has changed.

Some of the reorganisation of the church may have made things better, but no amount of reorganisation is going to turn a declining church into a growing one. And those who pin their hopes of salvation on a union of the churches would find, should they ever succeed, that that doesn't work either. There is good evidence to support the view that it would be a change very much for the worse.

Change, of course, is always with us. We live in an age of rapid change. Sixteen years ago I got the latest new thing in word processors, and now it is obsolete. I've had to get a new one. How long will that last? The things my grandchildren take for granted, computers, the internet, e-mail, TV, video, fridges, freezers, microwave ovens, transistors and even biro pens have all been invented or developed in my lifetime. I could name a dozen more – like tote-bags and sellotape. *Tempora mutantur et nos mutamur in eis* went the old Latin tag – times change and we change in them. But more in the past hundred years than in the previous nineteen hundred, and they keep changing, and so do we.

And so has the church, throughout the centuries and within my working life. It is only people with very short memories who think that it hasn't. The church's theology has kept changing, as people wrestle with the meaning of faith for their own day. The Panel on Doctrine recently produced a report on *The Interpretation of the Bible* which is the best piece of clear, straight thinking that I have ever seen in a church document. It ought to be compulsory reading. It is theology for the twenty-first century.

The church's worship has changed. If you could be transported back to a parish church in 1599, or 1699 or 1799, you might not feel much at home, with a sermon lasting an hour, and unaccompanied singing of the psalms. Organs and hymn singing were not allowed before the second half of the nineteenth century. Even 1899 would seem antediluvian. Worship today is far less starchy now than when I began my ministry 54 years ago.

Not every change has been for the better, but many have. Do you remember the frisson when the first woman took up the offering in your church? Do you remember the first woman elders, and the first time you heard a woman minister conducting a service? These are very good and important changes, and you don't have to be very old to remember them.

Some changes have come about because of social change. The cult of the popular preacher in the cities in the late nineteenth century was linked to the introduction of gaslight (in the church, and, perhaps more important, in the streets) which made evening services possible. And that ended with the coming of television. When poor relief could no longer

17

be undertaken by kirk sessions, the church developed its social work, to meet areas of need not covered by the statutory services. So things have changed, and go on changing, for reasons under our control and in response to social changes over which we have no control.

The church will go on changing quite naturally if we are concerned to meet the needs of people in this changing world. No one should expect the church to be the only unchanging institution in a world of rapid change. Yet we should remember that the Christian response to some of the changes in our world may be not so much to adapt, as to be critical of them. We should not be followers of every fashion. The fashionable 'isms' may have a short life, and the mature Christian will not be too anxious to join the parrot-cries when they need rather to be exposed as so much clap-trap. Christian integrity means that we must be men and women of our own age, yet never uncritical of it.

And we should recognise that the church should properly represent stability, a continuity with the past in a world where everything else is unsettling The church must always be reminding people of things that do not change, and the one who does not change, but is the same yesterday and today and forever.

Those who cry, 'All change,' are not very specific about what they want changed. Some ministers would like us all in T-shirts on Sunday mornings, singing mindless choruses, while they, dressed of course in jeans and a jersey, accompany us on the guitar and for the rest conduct a sort of chit-chat. That would be the height of modernity – the 'with-it' church.

I have attended services that aspire to that, and came away feeling that something was missing. The something was God. He doesn't get a look-in. From my own minister (who is not at all starchy) I am accustomed to worship that opens windows on the infinite, that shows me something of my own heart, and above all shows me the infinite grace and goodness of Almighty God. But in a 'with-it' worship we were left paddling in the shadows. The depths were not there.

But in the depths are the things that really matter, the things that do not change. Shallow modernising in worship throws the baby of reverence out with the bathwater of tradition. If we are not awed by the mystery of God, if we are not touched to the heart by his word of forgiveness, if we are not encouraged by the promise of his grace, it doesn't matter how formal or informal, how modern or traditional we are, the essence of worship has gone.

When I was provoked to think on this subject of change I searched the Bible and was disappointed. In Biblical times things changed so slowly that it wasn't a problem. But in the Old Testament I found the praise of God as the rock, the unchanging, reliable reality in the changes, the ups and downs of human life. And when the New Testament speaks of change, it is we who are being changed, into his likeness, from glory to glory.

Who is a rock, save our God? That is the word of the Psalmist, echoed through the Bible. Faith is based on the unchanging reliability of God. That is not to say that our understanding of God does not change. In the Old Testament there is change, as God's people and his prophets learn from their experience, and wrestle towards a deeper understanding of God and his ways with his children. In the New Testament there is radical change, as Jesus interprets anew the forgiving love of God, and is crucified for it, and as the writers wrestle to express the meaning of Christ and his cross. Similarly, within our own lives there is, or should be, change in our thought of God, as we learn through our experience and mature from childhood to old age. If at 80 my faith is no different from what it was at 8, I have failed to grow up, or learn anything for all my years.

Faith changes and matures. But God does not change. Since our experiences are all different and our learning never finished, our theologies are all relative. There is yet more to learn and unlearn. But that doesn't mean all are equally useful or useless. It is an error to suppose that because we don't have absolute truth we have no truth at all. We are seeking, however imperfectly, and some better than others, to understand the mystery of the unchanging love of God. With him there is no variableness, neither shadow of turning. Jesus Christ is the same, yesterday and today and forever. The fashions of the world will change. Even New Labour will be old some day. But God's faithful love can always be relied on, and will not change.

But it changes us. 'Love, love changes everything,' as the song says. God's love certainly does. Here we are not talking about the externals of religion, but of our very selves. This change happens when Jesus gets under your skin, when something of his patience, his openness to all, his caring, his faith begins to be formed in you. This is not an anxious desire to conform to any model, traditional, evangelical or modernist. It means freedom. Freedom to be yourself, your real self, which no one else can be.

'Where the Spirit of the Lord is, there is freedom. And we all … are being changed into his likeness from one degree of glory to another, for this comes from the Lord who is the Spirit.'

All change, indeed!

4 THE FAR-SEEING EYE

West Kirk of Helensburgh, 14 August 1988, to mark the centenary of the birth of John Logie Baird

Readings: Ezekiel 1:15–21; Revelation 4:6–11; Luke 6:39–45

Text: Revelation 4:8 *And the four living creatures, each of them with six wings, are full of eyes all round and within, and day and night they never cease to sing 'Holy, holy, holy is the Lord God Almighty, who was and is and is to come.'*

THE man of vision always tends to be an awkward customer. He has the far-seeing eye, fixed on possibilities that others don't yet see. He obstinately refuses to lower his sights to that limited world with which those around him are seemingly content. John Logie Baird was a man of vision. He had the far-seeing eye, and he must undoubtedly have seemed to many of those around him to be a decidedly awkward customer.

But that far-seeing eye, which in German is *Fernseh-*, and in English, through a curious hybrid of Greek and Latin, is *Television*, has been bequeathed by Baird to the rest of us, and it has changed our perception of our world.

I often think that the difference between me and my children and grandchildren is that I was formed into an adult before the advent of television. I can remember, as a child, our first wireless set. But I was in my late twenties before I ever saw television, and I was in my forties before I possessed a set. My children became accustomed to it from an early age, and my grandchildren could not conceive of a world without it. This single invention has changed our perception of the world more than anything since the

21

invention of printing. We are the television age. We are all now far-seeing people. Or are we?

Is it that television has given us the far-seeing eye, but not the far-sighted vision? It makes us viewers, but not visionaries.

This sets me thinking about two visionaries of the Bible, Ezekiel in the Old Testament and John in the New, whose visions have puzzled many who don't have their far-seeing eye.

Ezekiel's vision of the four living creatures, and the chariot with wheels pointing in all directions, so that it could go in all directions without turning, and the wheels within wheels, and the rims of wheels full of eyes, has defied the efforts of everyone to explain it. Even John the Divine, that later visionary, when he took it up and used it, had to simplify it. The best explanation I ever heard of it was by Dr F. W. Dillistone, when he preached in our university chapel some years ago. He suggested that Ezekiel, a Jewish priest in exile in Babylon, had been impressed by the technology of Babylon. This was something new. Not the wheel itself, of course, but the use and the power of wheels, whirring wheels, wheels within wheels, and he allowed that new technology to enhance and enlarge his vision of God. When you think of it in that way, it is almost as though Ezekiel might have been at one of John Logie Baird's earlier demonstrations, fascinated by the whirring of the discs, and the spinning lenses, which, if you weren't careful, might fly off at any moment. You can imagine him returning home from Frith Street, or Selfridge's, and writing, 'The four wheels had hubs and each hub had a projection which had the power of sight, and the rims of the wheels were full of eyes all round ...' and 'the spirit of the living creatures was in the wheels': indeed, because they could bring the living, speaking presence of the living creature into your living room.

Television has been called many names. It is, literally,

'The Far-seeing Eye'. But it has also been called 'The Evil Eye'. And John Whale, who became head of religious broadcasting in the BBC, called it, in the title of a book, 'The Half-Shut Eye'. We might also, with some justification, call it 'The Prying Eye'. There's no time to go into all these descriptions. Let me concentrate on the first.

In 1981 Richard Francis entitled a lecture to the Royal Television Society 'Television the Evil Eye?' The question mark is important, because Francis did not, of course, believe that television is an evil eye, and he, as Director of News and Current Affairs, was prepared to defend his journalists at the BBC and their colleagues in ITV against any such charge. While I would also wish to maintain the integrity and freedom of television journalists, I think there is one sense in which television is inevitably an evil eye, and another in which it can become one.

I cannot understand how anyone who watches television can fail to believe in original sin. If you are not aware of it in your immediate experience, television surely placards before you the reality of sin in the world.

I am not thinking of sex and violence, far less of unseemly language. Terrible as the violence and cruelty of the human race is, and we see plenty of that on television, he is a blinkered moralist who thinks that that exhausts the catalogue of human sin. Television can show us also the hypocrisy of politicians and the unctuousness of clerics, the banal vanity of chat show hosts and their guests, the greed of the great moguls and the vindictiveness of ordinary people. It can also, of course, show us the tenderness, the devotion, the self-sacrifice, the bravery and the magnanimity of ordinary people. When the far-seeing eye is showing us the world as it is, it is showing us the evil as well as the good, and showing us thereby the evil in our own hearts. If that is an evil eye, it is a healthful one.

When television depicts the reality of evil, tells it as it is, it does a service to humanity. But when it actively

23

encourages the evil in us, or pretends that that evil is good, then it becomes an evil eye indeed.

That possibility comes from two sources: the temptation to corruption within, and the powers of corruption outside.

The temptation inside is to sacrifice standards of truth and integrity for a criterion known as 'good television'; it is the tendency of the camera to distort, and for the medium to slide inexorably towards entertainment. There is the temptation for the camera to become the prying eye, which catches people in their unguarded moments and denies them their right to privacy. Those who work in the medium are, most of them, aware of the temptations, and they should be encouraged and strengthened and badgered to maintain their standards of integrity and truth.

But the temptation within is nothing compared to the threat from outside, from governments and from commercial interests, anxious to control the medium for the sake of political or financial power. There is a very real danger that they will succeed, without any effective controls left to maintain the integrity of television.

John Logie Baird all his life was struggling against the big barons of the entertainment industry, who, as he put it, had thrown their 'octopus arms around the entertainment of the whole world'. It will be an untold tragedy if his great gift to us is reduced to tabloid television; not a far-seeing eye, but a deceiving eye, which hides reality from us, an evil eye, whose God is pots of money.

At one time we had to struggle in this country for the freedom of religion. The struggle today, I believe, is for the freedom of the media, the freedom of information, and just as much as the other it is a struggle for the soul of humanity. Television has to be allowed to become the wide-open eye.

I have wandered too far from Ezekiel and from my text, and, perhaps some may think, from John Logie Baird. His genius, his struggles, his persistence, his vision have given us the means, the organ of far-sightedness, as it were. He got too little credit for it, and some of the things which he pioneered, such as 3D television, have yet to be developed. But what we see with the eye that he has given us is for each generation to choose.

Ezekiel had a vision of God. He was one of those Jews who had been taken by Nebuchadnezzar into captivity in Babylon. Many of them were saying, 'We are exiled, not only from our native land, but from our God. His temple is in Jerusalem. He is not here in Babylon. We are God-forsaken. How can we sing the Lord's song in a strange land?'

Ezekiel sees a God who is not confined to one building, to one piece of territory, to one nation, to one slice of life. Over all life, human and animal, he is supreme, he moves in serene and unhurried majesty wherever he will, and his eyes are through all the universe: the far-seeing, all-seeing God. Out of that enlarged vision, inspired by the technology of Babylon, was to come Ezekiel's message of hope for humankind.

Can we find any message of hope in a vision of God enlarged and inspired by the technology of the far-seeing eye?

It would be easy for me to wrap it all up by saying that if we give religion its place all will be well. I would not say that, though I certainly would say that the place of public service broadcasting is crucial to the health of the medium. But Ezekiel was not concerned about the preservation of the temple. He was concerned to give his countrymen a larger faith, that come what may, in Jerusalem or in Babylon, the far-seeing eye of the Lord was over all his universe, that he was not deceived, and that his purposes would prevail. The religious issue is not about religious broadcasting, important as that is, but about whether the medium is to be handed over to those who make money their god, or whether it is to continue to serve, however imperfectly, those values of truth and integrity, compassion and concern without which human life ceases to be human.

And the faith of Ezekiel, and of John, who, centuries later, made Ezekiel's vision his own, is that, despite the evil in the world, the far-seeing eye of the God of Truth cannot be deceived and his purposes must in the end prevail.

And the four living creatures are full of eyes all round and within, and day and night they never cease to sing, 'Holy, holy, holy, is the Lord God Almighty, who was and is and is to come.'

Television, like all the other works of men, must in the end glorify the God of Truth, whether we like it or not.

5 THE MICROCHIP AND THE PAPER CLIP

Readings: Ezekiel 1:1, 15–22, 26–2:1; I John 4:7–12

Text: I John 4:9. *In this the love of God was made manifest among us, that God sent his only Son into the world, so that we might live through him.*

RECENTLY I bought a new computer. My old one was becoming unreliable, so I took some advice and got a new one. But in 15 years the technology has changed and it has taken me into a new world – or, at least, on to the edge of it. I'm not yet surfing the internet, because it takes me all my time, and a considerable amount of frustration, to find out how to use my new iMac. I can understand that computer-rage has become a new problem in offices, with people kicking their computers! But I press on in hope. To take on this new technology at my age is, I think, an expression of faith in the future. I'm hoping that before Christmas it will have taught me how to do my Christmas cards.

These struggles, in old age, to come to grips with modern technology set me thinking about technology and faith. And I remembered the strange visions which Ezekiel, the Jewish priest, had when he was with the Jewish exiles in the land of Babylon. We read a part of his vision (Ezekiel 1:1, 15–22, 26–2:1).

He dates his experience precisely (28 July 593 BC, in our reckoning), and says that as he was among the exiles by the river Chebar, in Babylon, the heavens were opened, and he saw visions of God.

The exile of the Jewish people in the land of Babylon was a kind of ethnic cleansing, but much more sophisticated than that practised in the Balkans today. When Nebuchadnezzar of Babylon conquered Jerusalem, he wanted to ensure that that part of his empire remained peaceful. He took most of the leading families into captivity in Babylon, where he could keep an eye on them. He killed the royal princes and humiliated the king, and set a king of his own choice in Jerusalem. But the Jews rebelled, and the punishment was again severe, leaving only the common people in a land whose capital city had been laid waste and its temple destroyed. In exile the priests and nobles thought that all was finished, and that God had deserted them. 'How can we sing the Lord's song in a strange land?' they said.

But out of the desolation and defeat came in time a strange new hope. The prophet whose words were later added to the book of Isaiah began to explore the meaning of suffering and of God's purposes in it, and Ezekiel the priest discovered that even in Babylon you could still see visions of God. Strange visions indeed. 'The heavens were opened.' It is clearly a storm, and in the storm, darting like lightning, he sees four living creatures, each with four faces and four wings. These are the cherubim, the great angels of God. What interests me, though, are the wheels.

> Now, as I looked at the living creatures, I saw a wheel upon the earth beside the living creatures, one for each of the four of them. As for the appearance of the wheels and their construction: their appearance was like the gleaming of a chrysolite; and the four had the same likeness, their construction being as it were a wheel within a wheel.

The wheel is the basis of all technology, the most important invention ever made. The Jews knew the wheel, in a cart or a war chariot. But in Babylon they saw a more advanced technology than they had known in Palestine. Wheels doing man's work for him. These are cogwheels, machinery: tools that do what you want them to do. It is power. Ezekiel is excited by this, and so wheels within wheels, fantastic wheels, become part of his vision of the power of God.

Ezekiel is discovering a world that is vaster and more complex and mysterious than he had ever understood, and human invention adds to its wonder. But that doesn't lead him to throw away his religion as some do today and maybe did then. Instead he sees that God is behind all these things he is now discovering. God is vaster and more mysterious than the universe he has made. God is vaster and more mysterious than the inventions man has made.

My computer is the technology not of the wheel but of the microchip. I'm in awe of it, especially when it talks to me in a strange American accent. I'm furious at it when I can't get it to tell me how to do what I want to do. I know I use only a tiny fraction of its potential. I could spend a long life exploring it, except that in ten years it will be obsolete. But I don't worship it. It's not God. I know that it is there to serve me and not to be my master, to enhance my life and not to dominate it.

And I have taken great comfort from one small thing, which I early discovered. Sometimes my computer crashes. That is what they call it. I would say freezes. It gets completely stuck and you can do nothing with it. Usually it's my fault. But I discovered the way to unfreeze it, to get it working again. Something very high-tech surely? No. You take a paper clip, and you straighten it, and you look into the side of the computer where the flexes come out, and there's a tiny hole, and you push the end of the paper clip into it, and Bob's your Uncle, you're in business again. Believe it or not, these are the instructions.

When this piece of high technology gets fangled up, gridlocked, it needs a poke from a paper clip to get it going again. Something as simple as that.

I take that as a parable. From the beginning of time the human enterprise has tended to get fangled up, gridlocked.

Usually it's our fault. We've done something wrong, sometimes with good intentions, sometimes with evil intentions, often out of sheer ignorance and stupidity.

It has recently been realised that before ever the European arrived in Australia, the Aborigine was making a good job of destroying the wild life by his hunting practices. The North African desert is a result of the overproduction of wheat to feed the population of ancient Rome. Today we don't have the excuse of ignorance. We know that the destruction of the rain forest can produce desert and change the climate of the world. We know that the ozone layer is being destroyed by the emissions from our motor cars. But it goes on, usually because of human greed. Is there nothing that those who care for the world can do about it?

Again, take genetically modified food. Is this the latest technological benefit, or does it bode untold harm to the environment, to wildlife and to human health, and put us all in the power of the multinationals? The trouble is, we don't know, but the pressure on farmers and governments from these international companies is immense, and it is fuelled by greed.

Again, take war. War is always a sign of failure: the failure of diplomacy, the failure of governments to settle matters in a peaceful and human way. The war over Kosovo is a prime example. But it also shows us how high technology can go wrong, if a bomb aimed at Belgrade ends in Bulgaria, or another overshoots its military target and hits a hospital instead.

When the history of the twentieth century comes to be written it will be known as the century when technology advanced at an unprecedented rate, and human violence, atrocity, cruelty and slaughter reached levels never known before. We can put too high a faith in technology. It is only as good as human beings make it. Which means it is never perfect. And whether it is useful or harmful depends how human beings use it.

Like Ezekiel, I find science and technology exciting. I can thank God for the microchip. I can look forward to the day (though I may not see it) when computers will be so simple that even an idiot like me can use them. I can look forward to the day (though, again, I may not see it) when they will find a patient-friendly treatment for cancer. And I look forward to the day (though I may not see it) when we will build houses that will be heated and kept comfortable without destroying the earth's resources to make them so.

At the same time all our technologies are liable to crash, as my computer sometimes does. Sometimes the consequences are disastrous, as in war, famine or climate change.

Often the answer to the failure of science is better science, better technology. The microchip. But often the answer is the paper clip. In other words, things go wrong because we don't use them right, and we need a poke in the right direction.

And here I turn to our New Testament lesson. The first letter of John, Chapter 4, verse 7.

Let me read the passage again.

Beloved, let us love one another; for love is of God, and he who loves is born of God and knows God. He who does not love does not know God; for God is love. In this the love of God was made manifest among us, that God sent his only Son into the world, so that we might live through him. In this is love, not that we loved God, but that he loved us and sent his Son to be the expiation for our sins. Beloved, if God so loved us, we also ought to love one another. No man has ever seen God; if we love one another, God abides in us and his love is perfected in us.

The first thing I notice is the sheer simplicity of the language here. They are almost all words of one syllable. The most profound statement of faith is, in English, three

31

short words, 'God is love.' Unlike the language of my computer which I don't understand, because computer words don't mean what they mean in everyday life, this is simple everyday speech, used to speak of tremendous things.

When human life keeps crashing, frozen, gridlocked by our stupidity, insensitivity, greed and hate, God has injected something new into the world – he sent his son. He sent his son, so that in the language of a human life – a language everyone can understand – he might show us the things that really matter, the meaning of human life, the heart of the universe, the very heart of God.

He shows us love: his love for us, seeking us, forgiving the sins and stupidities by which the wheels of life get jammed, setting us free again. And calling us to love in the same way one another, for when we live in love – and only then – we live in God and God lives in us.

And that is why ordinary people admire those they see, aid workers, doctors, carers and people of integrity, who are breaking up the logjams that others have created, dealing creatively with the suffering and the mess of human wickedness and human folly. They are God's paper clips. For ultimately things go wrong not for lack of technology, but for lack of love. That was true when man was painfully discovering the wheel; it is true today and will be in centuries to come. And that is why Jesus Christ will never be obsolete, as my computer will. The microchip of technology will always need the paper clip of love.

Ezekiel's vision of the wheels shows how excited he was by new technology. But his final vision of God is not a machine, nor a computer, but a human being.

And above the firmament over their heads there was the likeness of a throne, in appearance like sapphire; and seated above the likeness of a throne was a likeness as it were of a human form. Such was the appearance of the likeness of the glory of the Lord.

A human figure. And though God is beyond all such imagining, and this is but 'the appearance of the likeness of the glory of the Lord', we find God in the human, in the one who has love in the heart. Above all we find God in him who in the sacrament thrusts his love into our hands and into our hearts, saying, 'Take, eat, this is my body. This is for you.'

6 FANATICISM AND FAITH

Readings: Isaiah 51:7–16; Galatians 5:13–26; John 16:1–7.

Texts: John 16:2 *You will be expelled from the synagogues, and the time is coming when anyone who kills you will think that by doing this he is serving God.*

Galatians 5:6 *For when we are in union with Christ, neither circumcision nor the lack of it makes any difference at all. What matters is faith that works through love.* (Good News Bible)

I once heard Dean Rusk, who was the United States' Secretary of State under Lyndon Johnson, being interviewed on television about his view of the twentieth century. He said that we think of the sixteenth and seventeenth centuries as the era of religious wars, and we tend to imagine that such things don't happen nowadays. But, he said, if we look carefully at the conflicts of our day, we will see how many of them are connected with religion: the conflict between Jew and Arab in the Middle East, the conflict in Northern Ireland, the strife in Sri Lanka, the war between Iran and Iraq – all, in part at least, religious wars. We could add the civil war in South Sudan, the Balkans conflicts, Afghanistan, Indonesia and South Timor, and others, I'm sure, where religion plays a large part in the conflict.

Dean Rusk then went on to say something which really made me sit up. He said that whenever he was responsible for Presidential speeches, he tried to keep God out of them. It wasn't easy, he said, because Presidents like talking about God. However, he kept trying, because it seemed to him important to keep religion out of politics. But can you keep God out of it? Can you keep religion out of politics? Ought you to try?

In the first place, we must have a good deal of sympathy with the feelings of Dean Rusk and others like him. The combination of religion and politics can be very ugly. The crusade is always the most ruthless and savage of wars. When the Ayatollahs first came to power in Iran we saw rivers of blood, ruthless persecution of other faiths, especially the peaceable Bahai, a long, sterile war against Iraq, and support of Islamic terrorism everywhere. Who did not then long for the common sense of a decent secular state? Reading about or visiting what people still call, without intended irony, the Holy Land, did you never long for the day when Jew and Arab would give up their crazy beliefs that God has given each of them divine and mutually incompatible rights to the land? As you see the efforts of well-meaning leaders to find peace there, do you not wish their peoples might lay religion aside and allow them to settle matters sensibly? Tell that to the Jewish settlers. Tell that to the Hezbollah. Because the conflict between nationalist and unionist in Northern Ireland was defined in religious terms, a fragile ceasefire leaves Catholics and Protestants still divided, and fearful of one another, despite all the peaceable efforts of the churches. In such places, does one not long for a decent civilised state, where the bitterness, hatred and cruelty of religion would be taken out of politics? And when I see the unholy alliance between conservative religion and conservative politics that is the Moral Majority in the United States, I sympathise with Dean Rusk wishing to keep God out of the President's speeches.

But is that really the answer? Keep God out of it? Should we be saying, 'Keep religion out of politics'? Should we not rather be saying, 'Keep fanaticism out of religion, and out of politics as well'?

There is a lot of fanatical religion around today, and not

a little fanatical politics; and when these two come together you have a particularly unpleasant and explosive mixture, and people get hurt. Innocent people get hurt. But the problem is not religion. The problem is fanaticism.

What then do I mean by fanaticism? After all, all religion should involve commitments, convictions, enthusiasm, beliefs you are prepared to argue for, some things you are prepared to die for. When does that enthusiasm, that conviction become fanatical?

'The time is coming', said Jesus to the disciples, 'when anyone who kills you will think that he is doing God a service.'

Perhaps there is the first mark of fanaticism. It is one thing to be prepared to die for your religion. Jesus himself did that, and many of his disciples. It is quite another to be prepared to kill for your religion. We don't read that Jesus or his disciples ever did that.

Yet throughout the Christian centuries the persecuting spirit, the spirit of fanaticism has been as dominant as in any other time. Christians have tried to deal with opposition to their religion by eliminating it, by silencing it, by killing it. The heretic, the questioner, the doubter, the unbeliever, the witch have all been hounded by the persecuting zeal of the different branches of the church. It may be by censorship, by legal impediments, by imprisonments, exile or by death – and usually a brutal and painful death. Those who kill them believe that they are doing God a service. That is fanaticism. A true religious enthusiasm will argue with its opponents, plead with them, witness to them, resist them if need be, stand firm against them, but it will always see them as children of God, precious in his sight, as souls for whom the Saviour died. Fanaticism annihilates its opponents as the enemies of God.

Why does religion turn into destructive fanaticism? Because it springs from fear and works through hate. Now, much human religion is based on fear. As Lucretius, the old

Roman sceptic, observed, 'Fear first made the gods.' Fear of an angry God, fear of an unpredictable fate, fear of a terrible law, fear of an ultimate hell. If we are honest, we will perhaps admit that there is a good deal of natural fear and anxiety within the religion of most of us. But if we allow that to dominate, then our religion becomes a sort of container for our fears, and then we have the kind of religion that hates any kind of change, that hates anyone who rocks the boat, that denounces anyone who questions or doubts.

It was this kind of religion that did to death Jesus of Nazareth, because he was opposed to it. Again and again Jesus is found inviting people out of their fear into faith. Don't be afraid, he says. Have faith. Your father knows, your father cares, your father loves.

For the alternative to a religion that springs from fear and works through hate, a fanatical religion, is the religion that springs from faith and works through love. 'When we are in union with Christ,' says Paul, 'neither circumcision nor the lack of it makes any difference at all. What matters is faith that works through love.' Put it in modern terms and you might say, 'It doesn't ultimately matter whether you are Catholic or Protestant, Baptist or Episcopalian, pacifist or non-pacifist, socialist or conservative. What matters is faith that works through love.' There, if you like, is a splendid definition of genuine religion. Faith that works through love.

But what has that to do with politics? A pure religion of faith and love, however attractive, would seem to have nothing whatever to do with politics, for politics is about power, it is about compelling people to do what they don't want to do, like paying their taxes, and stopping them doing what they may want to do, like stealing or murdering or terrorising. You don't do that with a rosary, as Martin Luther said. No, you do it with laws, and law-enforcement officers, and armed forces. What has faith and love to do with that? Just about everything, oddly enough. Because government based on fear and hate is tyrannical government, repressive government, destructive government. Where faith and love, trust and compassion are able to be present in the motives and the aims of government, then you have freedom. You don't have the Kingdom of God overnight, we should be sure of that, but you have a vision of a human society, a possibility still open and never closed.

But open only if we avoid the third mark of fanatical religion, and that is its terrifying certainty.

Some years ago I spent a night in the city of Worms, where in 1521 Martin Luther faced the young emperor, Charles V, at the council which we know as the Diet of Worms. Here was the classic conflict of conscience. Luther was summoned to defend his writings, and in particular those in which he maintained that popes and councils could err, and that many had erred. Charles was committed to maintaining that councils (he did not care about popes) had an authority which could not err. Luther was condemned, but it made no difference. He had blasted a great hole in the fabric of medieval authority.

Now I happen to believe that Martin Luther was right, and that the world owes an inestimable debt to his stand that day. I also happen to believe that the issue that Luther raised is still alive and important today. For what he was maintaining was the relativity of all human authority. Pope or emperor, bishop or king, council or parliament, general assembly or general synod, World Council of Churches or Vatican Council, all can err and have erred. It seems to me most important both in church life and in political life that we hold to that liberating truth of human fallibility, and allow no one and no thing, pope or prime minister, church council or economic doctrine to claim exemption from it. Then we might be on the way to a more peaceable and reasonable way of managing our affairs.

I find myself deeply divided from many of my Christian friends at many points. On matters of politics, from those both on the right and on the left of me; on matters of church policy and ecumenical politics; on matters of peace and war; and on matters of Christian doctrine. No doubt I must appear to them to be particularly stubborn, unreasonable, rigid and prejudiced. No doubt, in part, they are right. But I notice that some of these arguments and disagreements can take place with no loss of mutual respect, with good nature on both sides, and a genuine ability at least to see the other's point of view, if not to agree with it. There are other times, however, when we seem to encounter a blank wall between us, and there is no willingness to move, no willingness to listen, and communication stops. Usually quite literally, it stops. Because one or other of us has invested some human stance of our own with the ultimate authority of God.

But was that not what Luther did? No. Luther held not terrifying certainties, but humble convictions. He held to his convictions with awkward stubbornness. He was prepared to argue for them; he was prepared, if necessary, to suffer for them. But that was all. The rest he left to God.

But let me tell you the most charming thing about that visit to Worms in 1983. There, as in other parts of Germany, they were celebrating the five-hundredth anniversary of the birth of Martin Luther, in October 1483. In the great courtyard in front of the Catholic Cathedral there was a banner to celebrate the Luther Quincentenary, and inside the Cathedral you could find all the information about the celebrations. Honest disagreement between Catholic and Protestant surely remained and remains. But here you glimpsed the recognition that more important is their underlying unity in Christ.

What matters is faith that works through love.

7 THE FORTRESS AND THE FOG

University of St Andrews, Commemoration of Founders and Benefactors, 27 February 2000

Readings: Isaiah 45:15–19; Hebrews 11:8–10; John 1:14–18

Text: Hebrews 11:10 *For he looked forward to the city which has foundations, whose builder and maker is God.*

THANKS to Professor Watt we now have access to Walter Bower's *Scotichronicon* which contains an eyewitness account of the founding of the University. He tells us that in the year 1410:

> An institution of higher learning of university standing made a start in the city of St Andrew of Kilrymont in Scotland when Henry de Wardlaw was the Bishop of St Andrews and James Bisset was the Prior there. Master Laurence de Lindores was the first to begin lecturing there on the fourth book of the *Sentences*, Master Richard Cornell on decrees in the same faculty in the mornings. They continued their lectures for two and a half years before the confirmation of the privileges. [NB: The privileges he mentions were the letters or bulls from Pope Benedict XIII in Aragon, authorising the University to grant degrees.] At last on 3 February [that is, 1414] the bearer of the privileges, Henry de Ogilvie, MA, arrived in the city of St Andrews. On his happy arrival a peal of all the city's churches was sounded. The next day, that is the following Sunday, at the ninth hour there was a formal meeting of all the clergy in the refectory when the bulls of privileges were presented to the Lord Bishop as Chancellor of

this gracious University. When the bulls had been read out before everybody, the clergy and convent processed to the high altar singing the *Te Deum laudamus* in harmonious voice. When this had been sung and everyone was on bended knee, the Bishop of Ross pronounced the versicle of the Holy Spirit and the collect *Deus qui corda*. They spent the rest of this day in boundless merrymaking and kept large bonfires burning in the streets and open spaces of the city while drinking wine in celebration.

I like the reference to boundless merrymaking, bonfires and the quaffing of wine. Townspeople as well as the students, scholars and clergy, it seems, rejoiced at the founding of Scotland's first university. There was strong nationalist feeling at that time. Scotland still had to fight for and cherish its independence. Town and gown rejoiced together at the foundation of the University. Town and gown have always belonged together here. Do they still?

It was, of course, a religious foundation. It could not officially exist without the authority which came from the pope. Its founders and teachers were all clerics. Scholarship was the possession of the church.

In 1450 Bishop Kennedy founded the College of the Holy Saviour, in whose chapel we meet today. Unlike the chapels of Oxford Colleges, this chapel was built on the street, so that the people of the town might come and hear preaching. They still do, and behind that tradition is the thought that learning, scholarship and theology are pursued not just for the sake of other scholars, but to enrich the minds and lives of the people of the town. A revolutionary thought then, and perhaps more so today, when some scholars tend to write only for other scholars, in a jargon no one else can understand. *Aien aristuein*, ever to excel, does not mean elitism.

Then came St Leonard's, and when that became infected with Lutheran teaching the thought police began to get alarmed. Freedom of thought, the right to question and to criticise, was all right only so long as it stayed within the strict limits of Catholic doctrine. On the last day of February 1528 Patrick Hamilton was burned as a heretic outside this chapel. One of the charges against him was that he taught that faith and hope and love were so connected that he who has the one has the others. It was Lutheran teaching, and for that he was deemed worthy of death. Four hundred and fifty years or so later, I was reading one of the many books by the modern Catholic theologian Karl Rahner (of whom it was said that he never had an unpublished thought), and finding in Rahner precisely that truth for which Hamilton was burned as a heretic. Rahner died in his bed.

So, during the first centuries of its existence the University was expected to be the servant of the church, teaching and maintaining its doctrine. You may expect me to say that the Reformation changed all that, and swept the thought police away. The old thought police were indeed swept away, but it was not long before the new thought police were in place. From 1690 until 1853 every professor in a Scottish university, not just those in Divinity, but the professors of Mathematics and Natural Philosophy and Humanity and all the others had to affirm and sign the Westminster Confession of Faith, the doctrinal standard of the Church of Scotland. That was not to be questioned or criticised. The new thought police in the Presbyteries were gentler than the old. They didn't burn academics, and they didn't enquire too diligently what anyone, other than the theologians, was teaching. And eventually even the theologians were given the freedom to follow where their researches led and where truth beckoned. And the great nineteenth-century Principal of St Mary's, Principal Tulloch, was one of those to whom we owe that freedom.

So that's it then. End of history. A university today has freedom to question and to criticise, to follow truth wherever it leads. Or does it?

A university today is under enormous pressure – from a

vicious system of university funding and from commercialism. Today the ability to think, to question and to criticise is deemed far less important than the possession of some skill that the government of the day has decided is desirable. I'm waiting to see which is the first university to introduce a degree in Hairdressing, but my wife thinks that that has possibly happened already. Teaching and research are twisted away from the fundamental and towards the marketable. Research becomes a commercial rather than a cooperative enterprise. The thought police are still with us, though their demands are different, and their sanction is to take away the money.

What are the aims of a university? I am old-fashioned enough to believe that we must have freedom to seek after truth. Like jesting Pilate our age might answer, 'What is truth?', and not even stay for an answer.

Today we seem to be given a choice between what I call the fortress and the fog. The fortress is fundamentalism, of all kinds. Islamic fundamentalism, Biblical fundamentalism, Catholic fundamentalism, all are found in very aggressive mood today. They offer what I once heard called 'the terrifying certainties', and they repudiate with vigour and even vilification all questioning or criticism, however gentle. And many of the 'isms' of our time share these features of fundamentalism. I have never experienced such hostility as when in the company of some social workers I gently and innocently questioned the importance of so-called inclusive language. 'Political correctness' may be regarded as a package of current 'isms', which helps some people, especially politicians, to economise on the energy they might otherwise spend on thinking.

But it seems as though the alternative to the fortress is a fog. This is the view that since all our human cultures and outlooks are relative (and they are) they all are of equal value. The primitive animist and Augustine of Hippo are equally men of their time. Between the spiritualist medium and Mary Slessor there is nothing to choose. The witch doctor may be wiser than the most eminent medical researcher, and, because none of us has access to absolute truth, there is no such thing as truth at all. Many of my liberal Christian friends seem to find themselves in that position. We are left in a fog. If you believe anything today, except, of course, the dogmas of political correctness, you will be labelled 'intolerant'.

The extreme relativism which reduces everything to a fog produces insecurity. That helps to chase people into the fortress of the traditional fundamentalisms, and the intolerance of our modern 'isms'. In a fog, we all look for something to give us direction.

But the fortresses are idols. I'm struck by how fierce and scornful the Old Testament can be about those who worship things made by human hands. The one true God is above and beyond all that human beings have made or built. When you take any human construct, institution, book, creed, ritual, church or party, make it the foundation of your life, and say that it is absolute truth, beyond questioning, beyond criticism, you have created an idol. And when you do that you stultify yourself. And our fortresses are the cause of most of our wars, enmities and divisions. Those in the fortress can be fanatically cruel to those outside, and to those inside who dare to raise a question or a doubt. Theirs is the truth, and there is no mercy for those who oppose the truth. The heretic may not be burned today, but will be pursued, picketed and pestered as if all hell were let loose.

For my part – and I am a white, middle-class, male, heterosexual, Presbyterian, octogenarian Scot, which allows my views to be ignored, unless you count me to belong to a minority group, an endangered species – for my part, I find that there are certain things which I cannot deny to be true, and certain things which I cannot allow to be right. To give an example of the latter. I visited Glasgow's Museum of Religion (a temple of relativism), and found a showcase about Female Circumcision, presented as if it were simply an interesting custom, nothing more. I couldn't believe my eyes. To present this cruel mutilation from which women across so much of the world are forced to suffer as if it were simply quaint when it is morally abhorrent is relativism gone mad. I cannot be as non-judgmental as that.

I hope too that there are some truths I would be prepared to die for, if I had the courage of Patrick Hamilton, which I probably haven't. But there is a big difference between being prepared to die for your faith, and being prepared to kill for your faith. That is why the fortress is not the alternative to the fog. For the fortress is founded on fear, which issues in hate.

But supposing there is a place founded on faith that issues in love? On that faith, hope and love, which, as Patrick Hamilton rightly saw, always go together. The picture then is not a fortress, but an open home where the visitor is always welcome, where both host and visitor can be enriched by their questioning and their talk, even when it is quite an argument. You might call that the truly free university. You might also call it the inclusive church. You might call it the civilised society.

If the quest for truth, for deeper, more adequate truth, is not futile, it must be based not on the aggressive/ defensiveness of fear and hate, but on the openness of faith and love. On the oldest piece of hallmarked silver that the University possesses, the St Mary's Mazer, are inscribed these words from John's gospel, 'Grace and truth came by Jesus Christ.' Indeed, that is where they come from. Grace and truth. Faith and hope and love. That is the abiding relevance, no, the necessity of Jesus Christ today.

If we look for a city, a nation, a church, a university with these foundations, we may be sure that its maker and builder is God. And now to God, Father, Son and Holy Spirit, be ascribed by us and by the whole church, the kingdom, the power and the glory, for ever and ever. Amen.

8 RELIGIOUS OR SUPERSTITIOUS?

Readings: Isaiah 40:21–31; Acts 17:22–34

Text: Acts 17:22 *Men of Athens, I perceive that in every way you are very religious.*

THE Authorized Version of the text was 'I perceive that in everything you are too superstitious.' The Greek word can in fact bear that meaning, but most modern translators think it unlikely that Paul, who wanted to win over the Athenians, would begin his speech by insulting them. So they translate 'very religious' or 'uncommonly scrupulous'.

If Paul meant this to be taken as a compliment, he maybe had his tongue in his cheek. The line between religion and superstition is a fine one. So I might call this sermon: 'Very religious or too superstitious?'

In Arthur Miller's play *All My Sons*, Dr Jim Bayliss is a very sceptical character, and Frank Lubey, his neighbour, is very religious. The young man turns on the doctor and says, 'The trouble with you is that you don't believe anything.' To which the doctor replies sadly, 'The trouble with you is that you believe anything.'

Which of the two best represents our world? Ministers often talk about our modern world as a secular, unbelieving world: Dr Bayliss. But I wonder whether ours is not rather a world that is ready to believe anything: Frank Lubey's world. On balance anyway. To be sure there are sceptics around, who think that human beings are nothing more than rather inferior computers. But judging by what one sees and hears in the papers and on TV, there are lots of people, and lots of them young, who seem ready to believe anything, or almost anything.

The horoscopes in papers and magazines are read by millions. Some years ago I was shocked to discover, teaching a fairly large class in St Mary's, that I was the only person in the room who didn't know under which sign of the zodiac I had been born. They all knew, and they told me mine – Aquarius (I think!). My young brother was in the Merchant Navy during the war and he touched cold iron whenever he saw a clergyman. He had a hard time in Edinburgh during the General Assembly. Serve him right, I thought, for being superstitious.

When my mother gave me a gift of a penknife, she extracted a penny in payment, for a knife cuts love; but when she gave me a purse, she put money in it, for an empty purse is unlucky. She wouldn't put shoes on the table, for that meant a row, she wouldn't walk under a ladder, she had a thing about black cats, and she thought 13 was unlucky. Father, being deliberately perverse, said 13 was his lucky number. All this was fun which we didn't take seriously, any more than Burns took seriously the superstitions he describes at Hallowe'en. But when people do take these things seriously, their lives are dominated by fear.

Faith believes that our lives are in the hand of a loving and reliable God. Superstition believes that our fate is decided by irrational and impersonal forces. Faith has one God, creator of heaven and earth, our father and our friend. Superstition has many gods. The Greeks had little gods who presided over all the different aspects of human living, agriculture, trade, war, making love. You made sacrifice to whichever god you needed at the time. And the Athenians were so scrupulous that they were afraid that there might be some god they had overlooked or didn't know about, and that he might be angry with them for not paying attention to him, so they put up this altar 'To the Unknown God', which gave Paul the text for his sermon. Very religious or too superstitious?

At the time of the Reformation both the Reformers and the Catholics were against superstition. There was a lot of superstition and magic around – witches and wizards and spey-wives and spells and such like. Magic is linked to superstition, for if superstition believes in luck, magic aims to control it, by rituals, signs, spells and so on. Being afraid of bad luck is superstition: magic is keeping your fingers crossed.

The Reformed and the Catholics were both opposed to such superstitions – some of which were older than Christianity and some of which were a perversion of it. But for the Reformers the worst superstitions were within the Catholic Church itself.

Protestants have always believed that God acts directly in this world, that we are under the care of a good and loving God and whatever happens to us we can turn to him in trusting faith. The task of the church is to call men and women to that faith. The Catholic Church has always believed that God has delegated his power to his church, and acts on the world through the church. That is why the idea of power is so important in Catholicism. So when the priest takes the bread and wine of the sacrament and utters the sacred words over them he has the power to turn their substance into the body and blood of Christ. When water is blessed, it becomes holy water and protects you against evil. So a whole apparatus of rites and ceremonies and holy things, used by the church, become the means of God's action in the world. And the saints, with their special interests, replaced the ancient gods. (St Joseph gets you through your exams.) What the Catholic Church objected to was freelance magic, outside the church. Its own magic was OK.

But to the Reformed Church such magic was the worst of all. Not only do we not need all these ceremonies and rites and hocus-pocus, but they are dangerous, for they take us away from simple faith. Faith is trust in God who has graciously come to us in Jesus Christ, who acts on us and in us by his spirit, and on the world by his providence.

A few years back I read in the paper about a report that had been published in the *British Medical Journal*. A 19-year-old man from Birmingham had fallen from a block of flats and suffered severe injury. He was making a good recovery when he had a puzzling setback. He contracted pneumonia. The source of the infection couldn't be traced, until by chance one of the doctors walked through the ward at visiting hour, and found the man's aunt liberally sprinkling her nephew with holy water. The water was taken away and found to contain the bacteria that caused the infection. The man recovered, but the doctors wonder if this may be a source of other infections in critically-ill patients. Superstition may be bad for your health.

The film *The Exorcist* has been revived after 25 years. The scariest film ever made. What filled me with horror was that many people took this superstitious film seriously. The *Catholic News* called it 'deeply spiritual', 'an honest film about good and evil as spiritual realities'. It led, I remember, to many books on demon possession and exorcism, in one of which the author, an Anglo-Catholic priest, seemed to have performed more exorcisms than most ministers have paid pastoral visits. There seems to be an element of supply and demand in these matters. None of this is deeply spiritual; it is simply deeply superstitious.

But I didn't come here today to knock the Roman Catholic Church. The point about *The Exorcist* is that it did reveal widespread religious feelings which can easily be captured by the most terrifying superstition. The world is more full of credulous Frank Lubeys than of sceptical Dr Baylisses.

In one sense Lubey is right. The world is full of mysteries that we do not understand. But if we do not believe that at the heart of the mystery is a living and a loving God, the God who can be trusted, then we are a prey to fearful superstitions. Where faith fails, superstition flourishes. Are we very religious, or too superstitious?

I was once at a conference of Church of Scotland ministers, and we had a communion service. The minister conducting the service lost the place and missed out one of the prayers. Another minister came up to me afterwards and said, 'Do you think we really received communion this morning? He forgot the invocation of the Holy Spirit.' I said, 'If you think God is denying us his grace because John Campbell is needing new glasses, you have a very odd view of God.' Spirituality of that kind is superstition, and lack of faith. When we think that if we don't do things 'correctly' God won't bless us, superstition has replaced faith.

Look at the way we regard the Bible. The Bible is the source book of our faith, the record of God's gracious dealings with his children, of the struggle of his people towards a deeper, clearer faith, and of his coming to us in Jesus Christ. But the Bible is a human book, a book of wonderful humanity. It is not a magic book, as some would make it.

One magic use of the Bible is when people open it at random to get guidance. One divine tried that in a time of difficulty. He opened the book and his eye lit on the text 'Judas went out and hanged himself.' Not finding that helpful, he tried again, and this time his eye lit on the text 'Go, and do thou likewise.' This led him to two conclusions. One, that God has a sense of humour – which is a great revelation, a great and neglected truth. Second, that to treat the Bible as a magic book is a silly way to evade the responsibility for making your own decisions.

I'm amused at our passion for dedicating all sorts of things. What are we doing when we dedicate things? Are we making them holy? Weren't they holy enough before? When someone has given a new pulpit fall or whatever, we are right to give God thanks for the generosity of the gift, for the skill and craftsmanship of those who made it, and to pray that we may have grace to make good use of it. But we are not changing the gift in any way or making holy a thing that wasn't good and holy before. If we start believing that, we're into priestly mumbo-jumbo. A church that has had the painters in it has not been desecrated by these honest workmen, even if their radio played Radio One all day. To rededicate it is simply to give God thanks for their work and skill, and offer it and ourselves anew to God. When we dedicate our offering we thank God for his generosity to us, and we express our desire that the money will be used well, which means paying the central heating bill and the cost of the minister's car, among other mundane things.

And we dedicate ourselves, for it is we who need to be dedicated to his service, and part of that service in this day and age is to lead the vague religious feelings of our world into faith in the one living and loving God, from whom we draw our strength and to whom we give our thanks and praise.

9 STANDING ON THE SHOULDERS OF GIANTS

Readings: Exodus 3:1–12; Mark 12:13–17

Text: Exodus 3:6 *I am the God of your father, the God of Abraham, the God of Isaac and the God of Jacob.*

WHEN I first received a £2 coin I thought it very attractive, with the gold and silver colour. I could make nothing of the design, of wavy lines and circles. But I noticed that something was written round the rim, and I read it. 'Standing on the shoulders of giants.' I wondered, 'What is the Royal Mint trying to tell us?' I knew the saying that a dwarf can see far if he is standing on the shoulders of a giant. I looked it up in my dictionary of quotations, which referred me to Bernard of Chartres, who died in 1130, and to Sir Isaac Newton, who said about his scientific discoveries, 'If I have seen farther, it is by standing on the shoulders of giants.'

I went to my bank, but the girl there (you never see a manager nowadays: I doubt if one exists) hadn't even noticed that there was anything written on the rim of the coin and could tell me nothing about it. So I wrote to the Royal Mint, and they helpfully told me that the quotation was from Isaac Newton, and was chosen by Kenneth Clarke when he was Chancellor, because the design of the coin illustrates scientific progress. You could have fooled me. But when I looked again I saw that the wavy lines could be radio or other waves, or even a double helix, and the circles cogwheels.

Standing on the shoulders of giants. It is a tribute to tradition, to the people who have gone before. But our technological world moves so fast, changes so rapidly, that it doesn't have much sense of tradition, and tends to debunk the giants of the past. The new saint is Diana, who died young, still looking for happiness. The new hero is Bill Gates, computer whiz-kid, probably the richest man in the world. With them around, who needs the gods and heroes of the past?

Yet the myths of the past still have power. A few years ago the film *Braveheart* set Scottish hearts beating with a moving, though historically inaccurate, story of William Wallace. The anthem sung at Scottish rugby internationals evokes the exploits of Robert the Bruce.

So, do we still stand on the shoulders of giants? Even in the computer age do we still look to the giants of the past, and draw strength from their story and their memory? I hope so, otherwise we would be very shallow people. All nations have stories and legends of the past. So does the church, more than any, have its stories of great Christians and the saints of old.

Of course all these stories romanticise history. They always show how noble and heroic our ancestors were. They always ignore how meanly or shamefully they sometimes behaved. Bonnie Prince Charlie, for instance, was no romantic hero but an arrogant and dissolute opportunist, who in the end saved his own skin without caring too much about his followers. They were mostly Irish and Scottish Catholics and Episcopalians. Scots Presbyterians were never on his side, for they knew he cared nothing for Scotland save as a means towards the English throne and Catholic power. Yet most Presbyterians today think of the young Pretender as their hero.

Similarly with Mary, Queen of Scots, sent from France to win Scotland back to the Catholic fold. She had no sympathy for, or understanding of, the Scots people. She is a sad, lonely, even tragic figure. It was her misfortune to confront the one man who embodied the very spirit of the Reformation and could put heart into the nation – John

Knox. He continues to be caricatured by romantic story-tellers and ignorant journalists, but he did more for his people than Mary or any of the later Stewart monarchs or Pretenders, who did nothing to earn or repay the pathetic loyalty of the Scots.

Historical myths can be deceptive, yet we need a history to tell us who we are. Today particularly, we need to understand our true history and to criticise or explode the misleading myths. And we need to stop being shamefaced about the Calvinism which gave our nation its moral and intellectual backbone – and could still. The Museum of Religion in Glasgow, and the new Museum of Scotland both scarcely mention it. It is out of fashion today, and it does not leave many 'artefacts': its legacy is in stout hearts and tough minds.

Sometimes it is the strangers in our midst – the English among others – who see us more clearly than we see ourselves. My son-in-law is of English/Irish descent, but having studied in Scotland and married a Scot, he can see our viewpoint and identify with Scotland – even at rugby internationals! He is a good reminder that loving Scotland does not mean hating England or the English, but rather the reverse.

Sometimes you need to be outside your country to realise that you belong to it. Some time spent in America showed me, not only that I am a Scot (they knew that and I knew it already), but that I am a European, and have more in common with the nations of Europe, whose languages I don't understand, than with my American friends, whose language I sometimes do. That came as a surprise.

Standing on the shoulders of giants means recognising your debt to the past. If we need that as a nation, don't we need it also as a church? We are not the first Christians that ever were. We stand on the shoulders of giants.

That belief runs through the Old Testament, as in the story of Moses and the burning bush. A nation that has been ground down in slavery in Egypt is reminded that they are the descendants of Abraham and of Isaac and of Jacob, men of faith who walked free and proud upon the earth. Moses is given his identity, and he is to lead his people back to freedom again. He says, 'Who am I that I should lead this people?' He is a dwarf, he feels, compared with these giants of faith. But he is their true descendant, he stands on their shoulders, and he will lead his people on the long journey of freedom, towards the Promised Land.

In the New Testament the eleventh chapter of Hebrews is a long roll-call of faith, reminding Christians that they stand on the shoulders of Abraham, Isaac and Jacob, of Moses and of all the others down the centuries who heard God's call and ventured out in faith. The writer lists the great names until he runs out of breath and time, and then speaks of the nameless ones, of whom the world was not worthy, who witnessed and suffered for their faith. Then in a change of metaphor, he sees the Christians of his day as athletes running a race in a great stadium, whose stands are filled with the great crowd of those who have gone before, shouting them on to victory.

Paul used the picture of a building. Jesus Christ is the foundation, and 'other foundation can no man lay than that which is laid'. But on that foundation people build the building of faith. Some build well and their work stands, others shoddily and it perishes. But the building grows, built by Paul and Peter and others through the Christian centuries. We build on what others have done. We stand on the shoulders of giants: of Augustine and Thomas Aquinas; of Luther and Calvin; of John Knox and Andrew Melville and Thomas Chalmers; of John and Donald Baillie, and countless others. 'Time would fail me ...' as the writer to the Hebrews said. This is our history, the tradition that has made us who we are. There are different Christian traditions. They have sometimes been at enmity with one another, and there are still serious differences between them. To some extent they complement one another. I remain a Presbyterian, and a liberal Calvinist, not because that is perfect, for there is no perfect church and it is folly to seek one. I remain in my tradition because that is who I am, and this tradition is an important part of the whole.

This does not mean that we are slaves to our tradition: that we mustn't do anything John Knox wouldn't approve of, or must believe everything Thomas Chalmers believed. The tradition is a developing tradition. Those who stand on the shoulders of giants see further than the giants saw, because they live in a different age, and look to the future, not the past. Our task today is to preach and live a faith that will meet the needs of people in the twenty-first century.

For that we may have to recover some of the things the giants saw clearly, that we have forgotten: the things that Jesus taught – God's love and forgiveness, which no one can earn or deserve. The gospel of God's transforming grace. I don't think many people know that that is what the church believes and preaches.

Paul said that whatever building we build, Jesus must be the foundation. That is it. And that is why I took for our New Testament lesson the story of how Jesus used a coin to illustrate a truth. There was a debate among the Jews about whether a patriotic Jew should pay taxes to the government in Rome. The Nationalists hated Roman oppression, and the mood of the people was increasingly with them. The Pharisees and the Sadduccees had an accommodation with Rome which allowed them limited freedom within the temple, leaving larger issues reserved to Rome. They were satisfied with that, and they didn't want to go farther, or to rock the boat. But in spite of their control of the media they weren't doing too well in the opinion polls.

Then there was Jesus, a kind of loose cannon, preaching that God is our Father, who loves and forgives; who called men into a way of truth and love. It was easy for the other parties to unite against him, and try a dirty trick, of the kind we've seen often in election broadcasts. 'Is it lawful to pay taxes to Caesar or not?' The newsmen are waiting for an answer. Taxes are always a sore point. To accuse the other side of putting up taxes is always a good ploy in an election. Even if it's untrue, it produces fear, and lies and fear move the mob more surely than honesty and love.

Here the dirty trick is that if Jesus says 'Yes' he sides with the establishment, and will be very unpopular with the crowd, and if he says 'No', he sides with the nationalists, and is guilty of treason against Rome. Either way, they've got him. Wearily, he asks for a coin. In the temple they had their own coinage (that was part of the deal with Rome), but in the streets and markets the legal currency was Roman. He looks at it: the symbol of Roman power and Roman oppression, but of Roman peace and Roman justice and Roman roads as well. 'Whose face and name is this?' Then as now no coin failed to have the face and name of the monarch. 'Caesar's.' 'Then give back to Caesar what is his own: but give to God what is God's.'

For the time being he has slipped the trap. But in so doing he reminds us, I hope, that though we may be proud of being Scots, or British, or European, or whatever we think we are, above all we are God's. To him we belong, and to him we owe everything. Jesus stands for honesty and love, and he is the giant on whose shoulders we must stand if we, and our nation, are to see our way into the twenty-first century.

10 THE WORK OF GOD

Readings: Isaiah 63:7–14; Romans 5:1–5; John 6:25–35

Text: John 6:28–29 *Then they said to him, 'What must we do, to be doing the works of God?' Jesus answered them, 'This is the work of God, that you believe in him whom he has sent.'*

THE first version of this sermon was preached in Iona Abbey. I was attending a conference organised by the Society, Religion and Technology project. There was a youth group also there that week, and it was decreed that between us we should organise a service. A committee was formed, and, since I was the only minister in either group, I got to preach the sermon, at about twenty-four hours' notice, in the midst of a busy and demanding conference. No one but me seemed to think this odd. It may, however, have influenced my choice of text.

For one mark of the church today, not least in its best people and most concerned movements, is its activism. There seems no end to the people who are telling us what we must do to be doing the works of God. There are always new programmes and projects that we are asked to get into. I don't know whether this is in response to an unspoken demand from the congregations, asking, 'What must we do?', or whether, as I suspect, they are imposed on the congregations and Presbyteries by committees and officials who dream up new programmes because they think, 'We ought to be doing something.'

This is not entirely new. The twentieth century has seen an amazing succession of movements seeking to do the work of God. In the 1920s and 1930s there was the Forward Movement. I was too young to be involved in that, but I knew some older ministers who had been committed to it, and I know that it produced some good literature. After the Second World War there were Christian Commando Campaigns – a somewhat unfortunate model, since it suggested that the parish and the pub were enemy-occupied territory. But the church as a whole began to benefit from ideas that had originated in Govan, with George MacLeod. Visitation Evangelism and the Tell Scotland Movement sprang from this. We had Billy Graham and his Crusades. Since it was at that time that the churches started losing members, the years since then have seen a proliferation of movements and programmes designed to deal with the problem of declining numbers. We have St Ninian's, Crieff, offering to train everyone. We have Advisers in Evangelism. One year some ex-moderators issued *An Urgent Call to the Church*. We had Stewardship campaigns, an American import that did a lot of good until the spiritual aspects of it were neglected, and it became simply a means of raising money. We had adult Christian education and elders' training courses, which were warmly and enthusiastically supported. We have had Reappraisal for Mission and other programmes whose names I cannot remember. We now even have Franklin Graham, son of Billy, trying to keep that approach alive.

I don't want to rubbish all of this well-intentioned effort, in much of which I was myself involved. The Tell Scotland movement, picking up what George MacLeod had done in Govan and, later, Tom Allan in Kelvinside, engendered a good response from the congregations, who began, gingerly, to visit their parishes. The weakness of the movement was its lack of theology. No one seemed to have asked, 'What do we tell Scotland, other than "Please come back to church"?' The experience of the people would have led naturally into a second and deeper phase of the movement, but the coming of Billy Graham stopped all that, and people were encouraged to believe that the evangelisation of Scotland would be done, not by the people of the church, but by the 'magic helper' from across the water, with his simplistic, individualistic message.

One initiative I have not mentioned is the Society, Religion and Technology Project. It is not a work of evangelism. It is concerned to help the church think through its relationship to a ceaselessly changing technological society. It has been outstandingly successful, and has been much admired by other churches.

No one can complain that the church has not been seeking to do the works of God. But the result of all this activity is much confusion, and the influence and numbers of the church continue to decline. There are, of course, social and cultural reasons for the decline in all the churches, and perhaps they would have declined even more if we hadn't been doing all these things. Maybe, but it is salutary to turn to the answer Jesus gave to the question 'What must we do to be doing the works of God?' 'This is the work of God, that you believe in him whom he has sent.'

The Jews ask about the works of God, in the plural. Some of our translations obscure this. The Jews want to know what are the things they ought to be doing, to please God. The answer they get is in the singular. 'This is the work of God, that you believe.' They are serious about their religion. They are prepared to turn their hands to anything, to spare no effort, to accept any inconvenience, in order to get it right. What must we do? And the answer is 'Believe'. That is what God wants. Faith is the work of God: faith in Jesus as the one whom he has sent.

The question of the Jews is the question that all religions ask, from the most primitive to the most sophisticated. But almost always it is with this in mind. What are we to do to make God pleased with us, to make sure he won't punish us, to get him on our side? The answers have been you must offer sacrifices (sometimes even human sacrifice), or you must say the right prayers in the right places at the right times, or you must do without certain things, foods that are taboo, or you must do whatever the priest tells you, or you must go to church and you mustn't have fun on Sundays. When the question is answered in any of these ways it is usually saying, 'This is what God requires before he will love and accept you.'

The religion of works, or the religion of 'If' is the commonest religion of mankind, and I suspect that within the churches today it is the commonest religious assumption. 'God will love you if ...' is the natural religion of the irreligious, and of many of the religious too. I'm afraid ministers have perpetrated it for years in those dreadful children's addresses which always end in a moral. 'Now boys and girls ...' If the only Christian message many young people ever heard was 'Be good', if they were taught that as the central message of Christianity, can we blame them for getting along without it?

I think things are beginning to change now, thank God, if I can judge by what I myself am hearing. For it is not only children who hear moralistic children's addresses. Adults listen too, and seem to approve. So if for too long the children's sermon has preached 'Be good', the adults too come to believe that that is the essence of Christianity, no matter what Biblical exposition is in the sermon.

The problem with the religion of 'If' is that at its back is fear and anxiety. For if you believe that God will love you if you're good, you have always the anxiety that he won't love you if you fail, or slip up in any way. Then being good, or a good church member, becomes a chore. I've often been amused at elders' conferences and such like, to hear people complaining about those who don't come to church, or don't support its organisations. It's not that they're sorry for these people, because they are missing such a lot: they're not having the joy of worship, the warmth of friendship, the broadening of vision that the church can provide. No, they're not sorry for them. They're angry with them, because they are having an easier time than we are. The religion of 'If' leads to activity that is uncreative, obsessive, censorious.

Most religion, natural religion, says, 'God will love you if ...' Christian faith says, 'God loves you, therefore ...' The work of God, the first work, the fundamental work, is that we believe. It is a strange kind of work, because it is not something we do, achieve, or accomplish. It is something we receive, accept, to which we simply open ourselves. 'Faith is the realisation of the fact that one is loved,' said Kagawa, the great Japanese Christian. If this is the work of God, it is unlike other work in that it is not an anxious performance, but an abandonment, a giving up of anxieties, a trust, a liberation, the realisation of the fact that we are loved. It is faith in Jesus, the friend of sinners, who was sent to press the love of God into our hands and into our hearts and into our heads, saying, 'Have faith. Believe. Believe.' The work of God is that you believe.

I am not suggesting that in a world of pain and injustice all we have to do is sit back, fold our hands and believe. (Though sometimes that may be all we can do. Waiting can be a work of faith.) Nor am I suggesting that what we need is more spirituality. There has been a fashion in spirituality in recent years, some of which may be healthful, but too much, I fear, is an attempt to exorcise our fears and anxieties rather than to express our faith.

And there, I think, I have touched on the test of all our activities. Do they spring, joyfully and hopefully and lovingly from our faith in the unfailing love of God in Jesus Christ, or are they the product of our fears and our anxieties? Too much of our restless activity in the church seems to be a response to someone who is shouting, 'Don't just stand there: do something!' So we act – because any kind of activity seems better than doing nothing. We act – to exorcise our doubts and anxieties. We act, and we devise ever new programmes – because in so doing we justify ourselves and quieten our guilty consciences.

This is the work of God, that you believe in him whom he has sent.

But what flows from that faith is not a passive church, but a church more hopefully and purposefully and lovingly active. A church liberated from anxieties, and from obsessive needs and from censorious attitudes. A church free to love and serve the Lord, and to love and serve all his children. 'God loves you, therefore ...' is the message of the New Testament.

It is happening, and I have seen it and rejoice. But it cannot start without faith in the gospel of God's unconditional grace in Jesus Christ.

This is *the* work of God, that you believe.

11 Unity and Tolerance

First preached during the Week of Prayer for Unity,
19 January 1961

Reading: Romans 14:1–23

Text: Romans 14:19 *Let us then pursue what makes for peace,*
and for mutual upbuilding.

THE observance of the Week of Prayer for Christian Unity, in the eight days from 18 January to 25 January, has been increasing in all the churches. The idea of the Week of Prayer, in its present form, began with a French Roman Catholic priest, the Abbé Couturier, who had an earnest desire for all Christians to come into unity, and a passionate conviction that without sincere prayer all our talking would do no good. So in the 1930s this started, and has been taken up by Catholics and Protestants all over the world. But the question arises: 'When Christians in different denominations pray for unity, are they really praying for the same thing?' A sincere Roman Catholic, for instance, believes that unity will come only when all Protestants and Orthodox submit to the authority of the Pope and return to the Catholic fold. An equally sincere Protestant may believe that unity can come only when Catholics and others abandon the errors, distortions and additions they have made to the faith, and the false claims they make for their ecclesiastical institutions, and enter into the freedom of the gospel, faith in Jesus Christ and in him alone.

How then can they pray together, if each denomination really believes, like the woman watching the march past, that

'They're a' oot o' step but oor Jock'?

One thing we cannot do. We cannot put our different convictions on the shelf for the time being and pretend that they don't exist or don't matter. That is falsehood and hypocrisy. I am not a very dogmatic Presbyterian, because I don't believe that church government is all that important. But this means that when I meet some of my fellow Christians who sincerely believe that church government is very important, indeed, it seems, all-important, I stiffen up, because I fear that this involves making something or someone other than Jesus Christ the foundation of your church. I react as Paul did when some came from Jerusalem to tell his beloved Galatians that faith in Jesus was not enough, but they needed to be circumcised also.

How then, if we have such different convictions about popes or bishops or Infant or Believers' Baptism, how can we pray for unity? The answer of the Abbé Couturier was that we should pray for unity 'according to the will of Christ, in his way and in his time'. I'm not sure if many of us manage to do this, for we all think we know Christ's will and way and time. But the prayer points the way, if we will take it, to a more tolerant approach than most of us have yet achieved. We don't have to abandon or suspend our sincere beliefs, but we are called to carry our prayers beyond our beliefs, beyond our present convictions, beyond what we can at present see, and ask for what we don't yet see, the unity which is according to the will of Christ, in his way and in his time. In other words, we are not asked to betray or be false to the light we have, but to seek more light.

In search of a more tolerant approach, let us look at the fourteenth chapter of Paul's letter to the Romans. Paul is dealing with serious disunity in the church at Rome. The things that divide the churches today are different from those that threatened to split the church at Rome, but that makes it easier for us to look at them calmly, and learn how Paul dealt with tensions and divisions in his time.

It is not clear whether the problems at Rome arose from emerging factions within the church, or because people were coming into the congregation from other places and bringing with them new outlooks and customs. Maybe a bit of both. This was not uncommon, as the other letters of the New Testament show.

They were disputing with one another at Rome. They disagreed about what they ate. There were some who had decided that earnest Christians ought to be vegetarians, probably because the meat in the shops had been offered to pagan gods before it was offered for sale. Others would eat anything, holding that the pagan gods were non-existent anyway, and 'a little of what you fancy does you good'. They disagreed also about the right days for worshipping God. Some wanted to keep the Jewish Sabbath, and perhaps also various feast and fast days. To them this was a precious tradition, while to others it was outmoded superstition, for all days are alike. To them there could be no such thing as 'a holy day', for all days are equally holy. The result was a church hotly engaged in argument. The group of superior, liberated Christians despised the others for their superstition and ritualism, while the others condemned them for their frivolity and lack of principle. It may have gone so far that they couldn't agree to worship on the same day, or to have a common meal together.

What did Paul do? It is quite clear what Paul's own views were on the two matters under dispute. As far as food is concerned, the Christian is free. He can eat anything he likes. Scruples about food are a sign of weakness in faith – the hangover of old taboos. As far as days are concerned, while he is not against the practice of regular weekly worship, and assumes elsewhere that worship is on the first day of the week, he is against any retention of the Jewish sabbath, and any observance of holy days, months, new moons, seasons, that smacks of superstition and fear, and limits Christian freedom. Paul makes no bones about that.

Right, then, what would you expect him to say? You would expect him to lay down the law, to make an authoritative ruling: to say to the vegetarians, you are wrong and must desist, and to the Sabbatarians, you are wrong and must desist. And that's the dispute settled. Isn't that the obvious thing to do, when one lot are right and the other wrong? But he doesn't.

What else might he have done? He might ask the ministers and other church officials at Rome to deal with the situation. We needn't speculate whether there was a bishop or a kirk session. There was some form of church government there. Paul might tell them to make a ruling, to secure uniformity of practice, so that the divisions will be obliterated. They should exercise their authority. Isn't that what church government is for? But Paul makes no mention of that.

Then does he look for compromise, a formula? We've seen this often in industrial disputes, when both sides are tired, but neither can give in. You then find some form of words which each can interpret in their own way, and so not lose face over it. Ecumenical politicians are very good at this. But Paul does not provide a formula.

Instead, he provides principles, the principles which are the foundation of true unity.

As I see it there are three: the principle of toleration, the principle of sincere conviction, and the principle of love.

The principle of toleration. 'As for the man who is weak in faith, welcome him.' Welcome the man whose faith is weak: the man who hasn't fully understood all that Jesus Christ can mean, who has scruples, and still much fear mixed with his faith. Welcome him. 'But not for disputes over opinions.' I think that means 'But not to judge his opinions.' 'Come in, and let us put you right.' That's not a welcome at all. That's what the spider said to the fly. You are welcome *if* you agree with us and will conform to our ways. But that is the kind of welcome most churches give to those who come to them, and maybe that is the reason why so few come. I would not wish to come into the parlour of the church if it means being digested, processed, turned into something different from what I am. Welcome the one who is weak in faith, but not to judge his opinions.

I once thought that Paul was saying, 'Don't argue with the person who is weak in faith,' but I don't now think it is quite that. I confess I love an argument, and I think most Scots do. But we must argue not in order to be overbearing and impose our views on the other, swallowing them up. We argue and discuss so that we both may find new truth. Argument requires mutual respect. Respect for the person, though not necessarily the view. Paul is pleading for mutual respect and mutual tolerance: we are not to force our views on the other, not to judge or despise the other.

But the Church must not be tyrannised by the scruples of a timorous section, a vociferous minority. In Galatia where that was happening to such an extent that the essence of the gospel was being obscured, Paul could be very firm indeed. There are limits to toleration. But he is equally clear that the more liberated Christians must not make the others feel that they are not wanted. The first principle of peace and unity is that we should be able to hold together these differences of opinion, acknowledging one another, each recognising that the other is serving the same God, and is answerable to God for what he thinks and does. 'Who are you to pass judgment on the servant of another?'

The principle of sincere conviction. 'Let everyone be fully convinced in his own mind.' Some people find it easy to appear tolerant because they don't really believe anything. To them Buddhism, Islam, Catholicism, Jehovah's Witness and Mormonism are all equally good and even interesting because all are equally unimportant. Toleration for Paul does not mean that kind of broad mindedness. We need convictions. To pray for unity you don't have to pretend that you are not a Presbyterian or a Baptist or an Episcopalian.

Tolerance is not the absence of conviction. It is the outcome of sincere conviction respecting others who also have sincere convictions. But what interests me is the element of individualism that Paul allows, no, insists on, in the Christian church. 'Let everyone be fully convinced in his own mind.' Everyone has a right and duty to make up his own mind. Before God, of course, before God. This is not the modern sentiment that everyone has a right to his own opinion, but that everyone has a right to those convictions which he holds, conscientiously, before God, in faith. If you conform when not convinced, you sin against your conscience, like Galileo, forced to retract his view that the earth goes round the sun and not vice-versa, but muttering under his breath, '*Eppur si muove* [Nevertheless, it moves].' Paul takes the example of eating. 'The man who eats meat says grace, and this shows that he is eating with a good conscience, before God. The vegetarian says grace before his meal, and this shows that he is acting on his own convictions, before God.' And this is enough. Uniform agreement is not necessary.

Now in the past, throughout its history, the church, Orthodox, Catholic and Protestant has always tried to maintain its unity by securing agreement, forcing it on people, and eventually casting out those who could not abandon their sincere convictions. This is the root of the divisions in the church that are so often deplored today. It is a supreme irony, and ultimately self-defeating, that those who hope to repair these divisions should use the same method that caused the divisions in the first place, and would cause division again.

The principle of Christian individualism is vital to the true unity of the church.

The principle of love. 'Then let us no more pass judgment on one another, but rather decide never to put a stumbling block or hindrance in the way of a brother.' Beyond the principle of toleration and the principle of sincere conviction goes the principle of love. I have to think not only of my right to live according to my sincere convictions, but of the effect my behaviour has on other people, on the people who don't share my convictions. I am not responsible for my brother's views, but I am responsible for my brother, not to give him needless offence, to help him and not to hinder him. Here a special burden lies on those who think themselves strong, enlightened. A man may be convinced that he has a perfect right to eat or drink anything he likes, for his faith tells him so. But his faith doesn't tell him that he has to eat meat on every occasion when there is a brother who would be grievously upset or offended. He is free to eat, but he is also free to abstain – for the sake of his brother. There are occasions when love must limit freedom. For none of us lives to himself alone. The chief principle of unity is the love which looks to the other's good, the good of the person who disagrees with us; the love which expresses itself in constant consideration, courtesy, patience and forbearance and a deep and true helpfulness. If we would pray for and seek unity within our congregations and communities, and in the larger church, it is this above all that we must follow after, for it is the very spirit of Christ in whom alone we are one.

Let us then pursue what makes for peace and mutual upbuilding.

12 UNITY AND LOVE

Preached at the centenary of St Stephen's Church, Inverness, 19 October 1997

Readings: 2 Chronicles 6:1–2, 12–21; John 17:1–11, 20–26

Texts: John 17:22 *The glory that thou gavest me I have given them, that they may be one even as we are one . . .*

OUR lessons this morning are those which were read at the service of dedication of St Stephen's on 15 October 1897, and the text is the text from which Dr Mitford Mitchell preached on that occasion. The sermon will not be the same. I couldn't copy his, even if I wanted, for I don't know what he said. A hundred years have passed. The text is the same, but the sermon must be different.

I begin with the Old Testament lesson. One can understand why this was chosen for the dedication service 100 years ago, for it tells of the dedication of the first temple in Jerusalem.

Solomon was very proud of this temple that he had built. No expense had been spared. It had meant a level of taxation no modern government would dare to impose, and conscription too – forced labour. But then Solomon didn't have to face re-election. So the best of materials had been brought from all over the known world to make his temple the most gorgeous building imaginable.

At the same time, feeling that the earthly monarch should reflect some of the glory of the heavenly king, he had built a lavish palace for himself. He needed something pretty spacious to house all his wives and concubines and their children, and to impress foreign visitors. But these two projects had impoverished the kingdom, ruined its balance of payments, and left his people resentful and rebellious. Solomon was not all that wise. He was an improvident and spendthrift monarch.

However, at this point he is on top of the world because he has completed the building of his temple. In all its magnificence it is shining in the noonday sun. His temple. Of course he meant it for God, and now in the dedication of it, he solemnly hands it over to God. In the by-going he had built a large bronze platform so that he could be in a suitably exalted position for the dedication ceremony. The glory of God and the glory of Solomon seem sometimes to get confused.

'I have built thee an exalted house, a place for thee to dwell forever.'

Forever? Does he really think that this building of his is going to stand forever? Is he so drunk with the pride of his achievements that he thinks he has made something both perfect and permanent, and that God will live in his house forever? Perhaps he did. The great and mighty, the proud and powerful, the rich and successful often have that dream, that what they have done will last forever. It has been called 'the dream of the perfect act'. A vain dream, for it is never so. Shelley wrote a poem called *Ozymandias of Egypt*, about a huge and ruined statue in the desert, two huge legs on a pedestal, and near them a head with an arrogant and cruel face:

And on the pedestal these words appear:

'My name is Ozymandias, king of kings:
Look on my works, ye Mighty, and despair!'
Nothing beside remains. Round the decay
Of that colossal wreck, boundless and bare
The lone and level sands stretch far away.

Solomon's temple lasted about three hundred years before Nebuchadnezzar destroyed it. 'A place for thee to dwell forever'? No. Our dreams of the perfect and permanent are illusion. What we achieve is always flawed and temporary. We mortals cannot build to last forever.

That doesn't mean that we don't build to last, or build as well as we can. This building was well designed and well constructed. It has outlasted those who planned, designed and built it. May it last another hundred years, and another after that, though none of us will see these centenaries. Even so, it will not last forever. Nothing human does.

A hundred years ago the Kirk Session and congregation of the Old High had good reason to be proud of this new church. They had seen the potential for church extension, and had seen this fine building rise on what was then a green field. I think that that pleased feeling of 'Haven't we done well?' mixes with our thanks to God in all our celebrations. What worship does is to control our pride and deepen our thanks. So it was for Solomon. His prayers brought him down to earth, and he saw the limits of his own achievement. 'Behold, heaven and the heaven of heavens cannot contain thee, how much less this house that I have builded.' And he ends by asking God to forgive. We live only by God's grace, and in his forgiveness.

This church was not built as a temple for God to dwell in. Those who built it knew well that the God who created us all does not live in temples made with hands, that the God who redeems us meets us in any place or time. They built this as a home for the Christian congregation, so that they could renew their faith, their life, in worship and then go out through these doors to serve God in the life of everyday, in work and play and home.

That, I think, is why the New Testament lesson chosen for the dedication of this building is not about buildings at all. It is about love, the love of God, the love of the Father for the Son and of the Son for the Father, and his prayer that we should all share in that love and dwell in that love.

John's account of the last evening of Jesus' earthly life,

with its long speeches and this long prayer is quite different from the other gospels. John seems to be giving us the story recollected, with the meaning filled out after a lifetime of prayer and thought. He sees Jesus praying not only for his disciples, but also for all who in future will believe their story. That means us, though I doubt if John or Jesus would have in mind that people would hear these words nearly two thousand years later.

> I do not pray for these only, but also for those who are to believe in me through their word, that they all may be one, even as thou, Father art in me, and I in thee, so that they also may be in us, so that the world may believe that thou hast sent me. The glory thou hast given me I have given to them, that they may be one, even as we are one …

In 1910 Bishop Brent of the Philippines preached on this text to the World Missionary Conference in Edinburgh, and began the quest for Church Union and the long series of conferences, negotiations, initiatives and schemes which have taken place from that day to this. Church unions may sometimes be sensible and sometimes stupid, sometimes spiritually enriching and sometimes simply power-broking – just like unions of congregations – but to think that this text means that kind of union, to identify the perfect unity of love with the cobbled compromises and deliberate ambiguities of schemes of Church Union is to make what philosophers call 'a category mistake', to take two things that are on quite different levels and say they are the same. You cannot get authority for church unions out of this text.

So we will leave aside Bishop Brent and those who still haven't learned from his mistake, and ask what does this really mean?

It is about the glory of God which is his love. It is about God sharing his glory with us, that we may know the perfect unity which is his love.

Here we see the connection between the two lessons, but also the great difference between them. Solomon wants God to dwell in the glory of the house which he, Solomon, has built. Jesus wants us to dwell in the glory of the love which God imparts. Solomon's temple was sparkling, radiant, glorious with gold and silver and precious stones, a place fit for God to dwell in. Jesus prays that we may be the temple, people who shine with the radiance of love, people in whose hearts he dwells.

Solomon knew that his dream of the perfect act was only a dream. His temple, glorious as it was, could not contain the God who made heaven and earth. And Solomon knew that we live not by our own goodness, but in his forgiveness. 'Hear thou in heaven thy dwelling-place, and when thou hearest, forgive.'

But is it not the same with us? Is this prayer not also a dream of the perfect act? 'That they may be one even as we are one.' Can it ever be so? Can we sinful human beings ever know among ourselves the perfect unity of love that the Father has for the Son and the Son for the Father?

Some people seem to think that if you can just get people to agree about everything you will have the perfect church. But you just need to read the book of Acts or the letters of Paul to realise that in the early church there was plenty of conflict and disagreement. Because we are finite we are bound to disagree, and none of us can claim to have the whole truth. The unity of agreement is not the unity of love.

The unity of love is not the unity of agreement. You can disagree with someone and still love them. I disagree with most of my friends on something or other. Life would be much duller if we didn't have something to argue about. But we can still love one another. Most of the 'divisions' in the church are based on genuine disagreement, but we should still be able to love one another.

Love is unity: unity is love.

Life would be much duller if we couldn't enjoy and love

the glorious diversity and eccentricity of human beings. I sometimes wonder if that diversity itself is a reflection of the glory of God. And when we love and enjoy one another in our differences and diversity God dwells in us and we in him.

Maybe only when the Kingdom comes will we know it in perfection. But when 100 years ago this church was dedicated it was to be the place where we might learn more and more of that love and move toward that unity, and share it with others in this parish and beyond.

Thank God it has done that these 100 years, and please God it will do it for hundreds yet to come.

13 GETTING OFF THE GROUND

Service of Inauguration of the Scottish Congregational Church, 19 September 1993

Readings: Isaiah 1:1–4, 16–20; Colossians 3:1–17

Text: Colossians 3:1 *If then you have been raised with Christ, seek the things that are above, where Christ is, seated at the right hand of God.*

I was sitting in a train the other day when an aircraft took off from Turnhouse, flying low just over the train. I looked at this huge thing, and thought of the weight it must be, and the weight of the passengers, and the weight of their luggage, and the weight of the fuel in the wings, and I thought, 'How on earth does such a thing get off the ground?' Yet it does, and we see them above us, and we travel in them, and we have come to take them for granted. And I wondered if the Boeing 747, or whatever it was, should be regarded as a modern symbol of the church. How does the church ever get off the ground, cumbered as it is with such a weight of traditional baggage, and a great many passengers. The church should be a flying machine, but often it seems to be stuck on the runway.

The thing that had sparked me off thinking about the church in this way was something Denis Healey said one Sunday ago on the wireless. They were talking about the involvement of the churches – Catholic, Orthodox and, of course, Muslim – in the conflict in former Yugoslavia. Healey said that whenever Christians organised themselves into denominations, they become political institutions. I may not have got his words accurately, but I'm sure he used the word 'political'. I would rather have used the word 'worldly'. Churches are human worldly institutions, and as worldly institutions they use political power to secure their survival, or their dominance, to protect their freedom or their privileges. They tend to behave in the same way, and to use the same methods, as other worldly institutions do.

But that is not the way most preachers talk about the church, that wonderful and sacred mystery, the body of Christ on earth, the pilgrim people of God. Our writer to the Colossians is particularly fond of calling the church 'the body of Christ'. There are many other images in the New Testament, but they all stress that the church is not just another piece of the world, but is in this world as the body of Christ, the church of God, the people of God, a colony of heaven.

How do we reconcile the two perceptions of the church? The church as the body of Christ here on earth, the church as a worldly institution. The church as divine gift, the church as human organisation.

Let me suggest certain answers that won't do.

It won't do to idealise the church. We may not ignore the fact that the church is part of this world, and uses politics and power to gain its ends. Sometimes indeed this may be to the glory of God and the good of his children, *but* we may not ignore the fact that often in human history its ends have not been those of love and truth and justice, but power, wealth, position, privilege, oppression.

That was true on a massive scale in medieval Europe. It is true today in New South Wales, where the small Presbyterian Church, a splinter of its former self, is engaged in a heresy trial against one of its ministers, because he suggested that Paul, if it was Paul, might have made a mistake. It is true, says Denis Healey, of the churches in former Yugoslavia, condoning violence and ethnic cleansing.

We must not idealise the church. We may not ignore, as some church historians and High Churchmen do, the appalling crimes and failures of the church throughout the centuries.

Equally, we must not idealise the small congregation. The churches to which the letters of the New Testament were written were local churches: a larger organisation did not exist. And the problem is there in the local churches of the New Testament, for it is in these very churches that Paul and the others find the worst problems of unchristian behaviour and unchristian attitudes. Think of the church at Corinth.

In my own experience – and I'm sure in yours – a large church gathering such as an assembly, may be at times inspiring, seeming to take off in the power of the Spirit, and at other times depressing, seeming to express every feeling save those of faith and hope and love. In my own experience – and I'm sure in yours – a small congregation may at times be a warm foretaste of the Kingdom of God's love, and at other times a clique or club, dominated more by prejudice and pride than by love and service. The tension between the church as it is and the church as it is meant to be, the church in flight and the church on the ground, is to be found at every level of the church's life.

Nor should we delude ourselves by believing that when church unity is achieved, in the one great church which is some people's vision of the future, the Kingdom of God will be here, and all will be well. I cannot forget that the worst spiritual tyranny the world has ever known was under the medieval church and its inquisition, when there was one united church in Europe. I am not enthusiastic about ushering in again the possibility of such a blight on the human spirit.

So how do we reconcile the two perceptions of the church?

It seems to me that the church must always be both a human institution and a divine reality. As a human institution it has to work as other organisations do – and it has to be as efficient and businesslike in its operations as any other organisation. The fact that we are Christian is no excuse for incompetence. As a human institution we have to relate to other human institutions, especially to government and local government, and we have to do that realistically – understanding how to influence governments. As a human institution we need money, and we need to handle our money in a responsible and businesslike way.

As a human institution too, we are liable to become bureaucratic, in the bad sense, run by people more interested in the rules and regulations than in the realities. Like other human groups we can be hijacked by those who want power. What you have seen in political parties – for example, the attempt of Militant to take over the Labour Party – can happen in the church, where a small determined group can scheme to get all the positions of power and influence. And like other human groups, we can become so concerned with our internal struggles, or with our rules, or with our balance-books that we forget the reason why we are in business in the first place.

The Church of Scotland is facing a financial crisis. That has been rubbed into us in Presbytery and General Assembly this year, in an atmosphere of gloom and doom. That the crisis is serious there is no doubt. The Church of Scotland has been losing about 17,500 members every year for nearly forty years – since 1955, to be precise, which, coincidentally, was the year of the first Billy Graham All-Scotland Crusade. That seems to me to be the root of the financial crisis, and has needed to be urgently addressed. But the response which is been offered us is 'Cut public expenditure' rather than 'Meet human need'. Bureaucrats, who regard the church as a business, are inclined to want to close down the branches that are not making sufficient profit, and, when that is the spirit of management, the branches begin to get discouraged, for everyone has forgotten what we are here for in the first place. The church has to be businesslike, but it is always more than a business: it has to be and behave like the people of God, the body of Christ here on earth, the agent of God's love to his children.

The New Testament writers have a way of reminding the churches of what God has done for them in Christ, that they are now sons and daughters of God, imbued with his Spirit, the very body of Christ here on earth. And then they say, 'Why are you not living up to that?' 'If with Christ you died to the elemental spirits of the universe, why do you live as if you still belong to the world?' (Colossians 2:20)

The New Testament ethic has been summed up as 'Become what you are'.

> You are the sons and daughters of God, brothers and sisters of Jesus Christ. Live like sons and daughters of God, brothers and sisters of Jesus Christ. If then you have been raised with Christ, seek the things that are above, where Christ is, seated at the right hand of God. Set your minds on things that are above, not on things that are on earth.

And as you can see from our passage, the things that are above are compassion, kindness, generosity, love, while the things that are below are selfishness, lying, greed and lust. Getting the New Testament churches off the ground was not always an easy matter. The old ways still had a very strong hold on the new Christians, a force of gravity pulling them down.

How on earth does a Boeing 747 ever get off the ground? You don't say, 'Well, we'd be lighter if we reduced the number of passengers.' (At a rate of 17,500 a year?) You don't say, 'We'd better cut the number of the crew and leave it to the passengers to pilot the ship.' (As one writer seemed to suggest in a recent number of *Life and Work*.) You don't say, 'We could throw out the baggage and jettison the fuel.' (Away with theology and turn worship into a playgroup with mindless choruses.) All these things would make the aircraft lighter, trivialise it indeed, but less likely than ever to get off the ground.

What gets the aircraft off the ground is a surge of power.

For the church that power is the power of love, love to God and love to our fellows. What generates that surge of power is the good news of God's love to us in Christ. Where that is preached and that is believed, things happen. What generates that surge of power is the realisation that Christ who was crucified is risen, is alive, and has the power to raise us up with him. 'If ye then be risen with Christ, seek the things that are above.'

The glorious truth about the church is that ever and again this happens, and the church, whether it is a local congregation or a great assembly is lifted off the ground by the power of faith and hope and love. I think you had that experience here this week, when an oft frustrated dream became reality.

The sad truth about the church is that ever and again this fails to happen, and the church, whether it is a local congregation or a great assembly, gets bogged down in its rules and regulations, its wrangles, its prejudices and its fears, its sectarianism, its nationalism and its hatred of those who are different.

The sober truth about the church is that the church of Jesus Christ consists of sinful human beings living in a world of sinful human beings. The church is no angel, and it cannot escape from its humanity. It is a worldly organisation. But it is still this sinful, worldly organisation through which Christ does his work among men, and we may not reject it. The church *is* a wonderful and sacred mystery, and the mystery is this: Christ in you, the hope of glory.

14 EXCLUDING AND INCLUDING

Readings: Deuteronomy 30:15–20; I Corinthians 4:8–13; Matthew 16:13–23

Text: I Corinthians 4:8 *All of you, no doubt, have everything you could desire. You have come into your fortune already. You have come into your kingdom – and left us out. How I wish you had indeed won your kingdom; then you might share it with us!* (New English Bible)

I can remember the impact this verse had on me when I first heard it in this translation. I was familiar enough with this chapter, but never before had the smug superiority of the Christians at Corinth come across so vividly. And I began to think of all those I had met who could say, 'We are Christians', with the pride that implies that outside of their little group no one else is. I began to realise why I reacted as I did to all the true believers I had met, with their guitars and their smiling, self-satisfied faces. I began to see also why I felt frustrated with some good church members, supporters of the free-will offering and singers in the choir, who are less than welcoming to those who are not so well dressed and not so respectable. And I began to wonder about myself …

Paul is using sarcasm, which I hope was not lost on the church at Corinth.

> All of you no doubt have everything you could desire. You have come into your fortune already. You have come into your kingdom – and left us out. How I wish you had indeed won your kingdom then you might share it with us!

Here is the exclusive attitude (you have left us out); and the inclusive attitude (then you might share it with us).

What led Paul to be so cutting, so sarcastic, with the Christians at Corinth? It seems that having heard first Paul and then Apollos preaching about the grace of God and his Kingdom, they had come to the conclusion that they had arrived. There was nothing more they needed. They had it all sewn up. Nothing more to learn, nothing to question, nothing to worry about, nothing to struggle for. Spiritually, they were rich. They were behaving as if they had won a million pounds on the Lottery. There's no need to work any more. The only question is how you are going to enjoy all these riches.

So they said, 'We are the saved', or, 'We are the people', or, 'We are true Christians'.

One result of their comforting certainties was that they felt infinitely superior to anyone who had not yet arrived, and that must have included all those who found faith difficult and life a struggle and whose experience of following Christ was that it seemed to land them often in trouble and in pain. That would certainly include poor old Paul, who was stomping around preaching his gospel and getting more kicks than ha'pence for his pains. He gets beaten up, thrown into prison. He has to do manual work to keep body and soul together ... poor, struggling Paul, always, it seemed, at the end of his tether, in conflict with the civil authorities, in conflict with the Jewish authorities, in conflict often with his own churches, and no sooner getting one problem sorted out and hoping for a little rest when some new crisis would erupt – and once again, he's swimming out of his depth.

But these wise, enlightened Corinthians are superior to all of that. Their faith and their knowledge and their experience give them sublime certainties and dazzling self-confidence. True, they don't go out into the sort of places where Paul gets roughed up. They have a way of organising their lives so that the story is one of success, success all the way.

The only trouble they have is that which bedevils all exclusive groups – splits and divisions. There are already a number of groups in Corinth, and each of them claims that they, and they alone, have the real truth, the full Gospel, and that all the others are defective. They even gather around the great names – Paul, Apollos, Peter, even Christ – though none of the apostles has given any sanction to that.

So in Corinth we have the familiar picture of the exclusive Christian.

We are God's chosen few
All others will be damned.
There is no room in heaven for you;
We can't have heaven crammed!

The exclusive person is always happy to leave some people out. Indeed, there is no fun being 'in' if there aren't some people who are 'out'. For the exclusive person it is very important that those who don't share his experience, or his doctrine, or his apostolic succession, or his moral sanctity should be 'out'. 'You have come into your kingdom – and left us out.'

But surely it is the most natural thing in the world to form groups. The world is made up of groups, from the family outwards. Children seem to do it spontaneously. They form clubs and gangs and have secret passwords. It's all a game really, though you can have a sore heart if you are a little boy and your big brother won't let you join the gang. Adults do it too, of course. It would be no fun, I suppose, to belong to the Royal and Ancient Golf Club if anyone could be a member. The rich, it has been said, need the poor to look down on. Or, as Groucho Marx put it, 'I don't want to belong to any club that will accept me as a member.'

Some groups, of course, are formed because of a common concern: charities like Christian Aid, peace groups,

Friends of the Earth, political parties – and churches. These are formed on the basis of principle rather than privilege. Even in these the attitude of exclusiveness may creep in, when people stop listening to any voices other than those of their own group, when their opponents become their enemies. One could instance the difference in behaviour between animal rights groups and animal welfare groups. The rights groups show the destructive end of exclusiveness; in religion it leads to bigotry, sectarianism, fanaticism; in nationalism to war. That is where you may end if you follow the way of in and out, us and them.

'You have come into your kingdom, and left us out.' But can any kingdom that leaves others out in the cold, and is happy to leave them so, be God's Kingdom?

The opposite of the exclusive attitude is, of course, the inclusive attitude. Many high-minded people today are so turned off by what they see as the quarrelsomeness and divisiveness of sects and religions, each making exclusive claims, that they say, 'Let's recognise that all religions are the same at heart. Let's be inclusive. Let's embrace them all.' Something like that seems to lie behind the fashion for Religious Studies in schools and universities, and also perhaps the decision of the Scottish Parliament to have 'multi-faith prayers'. They don't wish to exclude anyone, so they will embrace all faiths. No one has shown me the numbers of Jews, Muslims, Buddhists, Sikhs, Hindus and others who are members of the Scottish Parliament. It seems to me that the Parliament is so anxious to be inclusive, that it is including a large number of people who aren't there. Or perhaps they were just being politically correct. I was cheered that they responded so well to Burns's hope that 'man to man the warld o'er shall brithers be for a' that', and that no one wanted to change the words to 'Person to person the warld o'er shall siblings be for a' that'. That is me being naughty, but it illustrates the problem of being totally inclusive. You end up being wet and insipid.

I remember once watching a religious programme on TV – something I don't often do. In this there was a panel and an audience, and there were two parents who had suffered the loss of a child to the Moonies – or it may have been the Children of God, or one of the other man-eating sects. Everyone was so anxious to be liberal and tolerant (including a good bishop on the panel) that no one seemed able to accept or feel the real pain of these parents, and no one could say, what needed to be said, that some forms of religion are simply evil, and need to be resisted. I even found myself longing for someone like Ian Paisley to give us some good old-fashioned religious bigotry. For religions are not like the different flavours of potato crisps. It's not a matter of taste which religion, if any, you choose. It's a matter of truth and falsehood, good and evil, life and death. It is a matter of the things you must stand for, no matter what it costs you.

It is one thing to disagree with a Jew as to whether or not one may eat pork. That is life and death only for the pig. It was another thing to disagree with Hitler and Eichmann, who believed that all Jews must be exterminated. That was life and death for millions of Jews. As Bonhoeffer said at the time, 'He who will not stand up for the Jews has no right to sing Gregorian chant.'

There are deep disagreements, there are matters of life and death, matters of principle, which cannot be swept under the carpet of a bland tolerance.

Now I seem to be saying that the exclusive attitude and the inclusive are both wrong. How can that be?

Because both behave as if we had God's Kingdom perfect and complete, and there is nothing more to wait for, or to struggle for. But if it is true that God's Kingdom has come in Jesus, and where his Spirit is, there is the Kingdom, it is equally true that this world is not yet the Kingdom; we grasp the Kingdom only in faith.

Nor is the church the Kingdom. That is part of the

mistake the Corinthians made. They thought they had the Kingdom already, in the church. It is that attitude that leads to sectarianism. Some in the Catholic community in Scotland complain bitterly about Protestant sectarianism and bigotry. Such bigotry as exists today, mainly in the west of Scotland, is the hangover of mutual resentment between an immigrant community and the native population, and survives mainly, as one of my Catholic friends pointed out, among those who don't go to church. How much healthier life would be in Glasgow if instead of Celtic and Rangers they all supported Partick Thistle!

It needs to be said that it is not only Protestants who can be bigoted. Alas, those who identify their church with the Kingdom cannot recognise their own sectarianism.

Those who scream 'sectarianism' fall into the temptation of those minorities today who use the claim that they are offended to evade all rational criticism of their practices or behaviour. We must not give offence. That seems to leave a tolerant society with no choice but to be so inclusive that they tolerate anything. We need to recognise that some religious practices are evil, and not be afraid to say so.

So, are we back in our exclusive boxes, dividing the world into us and them, just as Western movies divide the world into goodies and baddies? Only if we are bullied, by the cries of sectarianism and the claims of those who take offence, into abandoning reasonable and charitable argument about religion. I am not a Muslim because I believe that Islam is mistaken. I am not a Catholic because I believe that in certain things Catholicism is gravely mistaken. These are not differences that can or should be swept under the carpet. Religious debate can easily fall into the *odium theologicum*, theological hatred, precisely because these are matters about which we feel strongly and should feel strongly. In this torn and evil world religion cannot be reduced to the level of the polite conversation in a senior common room or some gentleman's club. It is a matter of life and death, of seeking the truth and witnessing to the truth we see, of standing for what we believe is right, though we suffer for it. As Paul knew, and his superior Corinthians had yet to learn, we cannot be superior to the Cross.

Yet in the end Christianity must be inclusive. On that Cross Jesus is stretching out his arms to a sinful and suffering world. Love is inclusive. The Kingdom is not complete so long as anyone is left out. And maybe that could point the way to a sensitive and Christian evangelism.

'How I wish you had indeed won your kingdom: then you might share it with us!'

15 AGE AND YOUTH TOGETHER

Presentation of long-service certificate, Carnbee, 6 July 1997

Readings: Zechariah 8:3–8; Colossians 3:12–24; Luke 21:1–4

Text: Zechariah 8:4–5 *Thus says the Lord of hosts: Old men and old women shall again sit in the streets of Jerusalem, each with staff in hand for very age. And the streets of the city shall be full of boys and girls playing in its streets.*

> Crabbed age and youth cannot live together;
> Youth is full of pleasure, age is full of care.

THAT'S not a text. It's from a poem called 'The Passionate Pilgrim', by William Shakespeare. I think for once the good bard nodded, for I hope what he said is not true.

But the view that Age and Youth don't mix is widely held. For a contrast I turn to the prophet Zechariah. In one of my favourite Old Testament passages he paints a picture, a dream, of a city at peace, of life as it should be.

> Old men and old women shall again sit in the streets of Jerusalem, each with staff in hand for very age. And the streets of the city shall be full of boys and girls playing in its streets. (Zechariah 8:4–5)

When I was a boy in Leith, the street was our playground. The girls played peevers on the pavement in front of the shops and no one ever complained or tried to stop them – adults going in and out of the shops would sometimes do a wee hop in the boxes, remembering their own childhood. The boys sometimes did too! But we played free-the-den, roving all round the streets, and we even played cricket in a quiet street, with a lamp-post as the wicket. I don't remember old people sitting in the street, partly I suppose because the Scottish climate isn't conducive to that, partly because Edinburgh people would prefer to sit in privacy at the back of their houses, rather than in public at the front. But in the East Neuk of Fife I've seen the old people sitting in the sun at their front doors while the children played in front of them. My uncle, who lived in St John's Wood in London, had a stroke which left him a bit lame. And he used to go out to what he called 'the burial', the churchyard, where there was also a children's playground. There he used to sit among the gravestones and watch the children play.

It is odd that the prophet does not mention the work that would be going on in Jerusalem – he concentrates on the very old and the very young. The signs of a peaceful, happy city are old people sitting and talking, and young people running and playing. Nothing about work. Yet that, of course, is going on. The street and the market place were public spaces where people met and talked and did their business and shared the gossip of the place. The smith with his forge, the potter with his wheel, the weaver with his loom, the carpenter with his bench, the tailor with his cloth, and the shops and the markets were all there, without doors or locks, and people would wander in and out, in friendship or on business, and the children would run around their feet, playing their games, and the old people would sit and talk and greet friends in the passing. A happy, peaceful community has a place for every age.

In troubled times, when there is war and conflict, the old people and the children are not there, for there is danger on the street. Old people and children were not to be seen much on the streets of Sarajevo in recent times, because of the fighting there. That is why Zechariah's vision of peace and prosperity involves the old people and the children: their presence is a sign of peace.

Has that kind of all-embracing community been shattered by our modern world, and lost beyond recall? Are we doomed to live in fragmented worlds, where Shakespeare is right and Zechariah wrong – where age and youth cannot live together?

At first sight the answer seems to be 'Yes'. That's the way the world is nowadays. No longer do people live and work and have their leisure and their family life and their education and their worship all in the one place, as a large extended family. The weaver doesn't now have a loom in his front room, or the tailor a table where he sits cross-legged. People go out to work, and children go out to school, often by bus to the nearby town, because the village school has closed. Farming above all has changed, machinery displacing people, and developers turning old farm steadings into groups of desirable residences for commuters. The new hamlet and the old village cannot sustain shops because everyone does their shopping in the supermarket with the big carpark on the outskirts of the town. As for the street, it is almost impossible to cross, let alone play in, and the petrol fumes make it unpleasant to sit in.

So life has become fragmented. Home, work, education, leisure, worship (if you still include that) happen in different places. We are all mobile, and our paths criss-cross. Ours is the consumer society. The supermarket is the temple of the modern world. We choose what we will do and where we will do it and whom we will do it with.

The young to the disco, the old to the bowling green. That might seem to be all that is to be said. And the church seems to have gone the same way. We send the young out to Sunday School and exclude them from the church service after 15 minutes. Then we wonder why they don't want to become communicants. We have shut them out from the adult services. What more can we do for our young people, we ask, and seldom ask what they might do for us if only we did not exclude them.

The General Assembly, and especially its Board of Practice and Procedure has been worried in recent years that we have an aging membership, and that the image of the church is an elderly image. So they put forward a number of proposals to make ministers retire earlier, and to make sure that retired ministers and elders over 70 didn't play any part in Presbytery. Some of these moves – for example to have an age limit on elders – have fortunately been frustrated. But the Board seems to persist in its pathetic belief that if only you eliminate the aged you will have a young and vigorous church. Poppy-cock. You end up with a middle-aged church. The young are not going to rush in because the over-seventies have been marginalised.

In 1997 the Church and Nation Committee produced a report on *Demographic Changes – The Third Age*. It points out that there are more old people in church today because there are more old people in society. In 1901 life expectancy for a woman was 49, and for a man $45\frac{1}{2}$. Today a woman can expect to live to nearly 80 and a man to over 74. These are the averages. But what a change! What a marvellous change!

The report sees this as an opportunity, not, as some think, a problem. The creative gifts and the human talent among those who are no longer earning are to be valued, used and cherished. The last paragraph of the report says this:

The church has always, quite rightly, emphasised the need to cherish and nurture youth. It has not appeared to celebrate the presence of older people ... If the church can be attractive to older people they will bring with them many gifts for the good of the whole body . . .

I would like to see that report framed and put above the desks of the Secretaries in all the offices in 121 George Street. And that brings me to the long-service certificates. For in fact the church does value long and faithful service, and the experience that goes with it. Most of you who receive certificates today were quite young when you started, and some of you are not so old yet. For some the attainment of a long-service certificate is a sign to hang up the boots and saddle, but some of you have a good many active years yet and I hope you will enjoy them.

We need to know, of course, when it is time to ease up, slow the pace. There is wisdom in knowing that. I remember when my old minister, Dr Arthur A. Cowan, was celebrating 60 years in the ministry, still active, though over 80. They all loved him in Inverleith Church, but some thought he ought to retire. As an anniversary gift they gave him a television, a nice hint that he could spend more time watching it. In thanking them he said, 'This is not the Mort d'Arthur', and indicated that he had no intention of retiring.

He was free to go on till he died, and he did. In that he was unwise, I think. I did not have such a choice, and I am glad of that. I can still do things for the church, but I am not in a position of power. I can exercise some influence, but I don't have power. That gives me freedom. I rather think that we who are old can better influence events if we don't cling to power. Our experience may be better heeded if we don't pose a threat to those who are younger.

There are more retired people in society than ever before. And there are fewer young people nowadays. The Church of Scotland is not alone in feeling the effect of this. Our membership figures go down, not because people are leaving the church, but simply because we are not replacing those who die. We need to cherish the young, and to ask seriously whether the kind of Christian education we give them is fitting them for a world in which the commercial pressures and the peer-group pressures are against Christian commitment. We need to ask too whether we let them do enough for us, whether we take them seriously enough.

At the General Assembly of 1997 two young people gave a report on the Youth Assembly. Many of us felt that this was one of the most refreshing and encouraging sessions of the Assembly. They told us what the Youth Assembly had been discussing, and they wanted us to listen to their views. Clearly they felt that they had been excluded, and so they have. But for that very reason, they did not wish to exclude anyone else. They had the vision that Age and Youth together might share experience, listen to one another, and move the church forward in the spirit of Christ. I felt that they brought alive Zechariah's vision for the peace of the church and for the peace of society.

'Old men and old women shall again sit in the streets of Jerusalem, each with staff in hand for very age. And the streets of the city shall be full of boys and girls playing in the streets.'

16 THE TOURIST AND THE EXILE

*(Opening service of the American Summer Institute,
St Andrews, 27 June 1976)*

Readings: Genesis 12:1–9; Acts 17:2–31

Text: Acts 17:26 *He created every race of men of one stock, to
inhabit the whole earth's surface. He fixed the epochs of their
history and the limits of their territory.* (New English Bible)

THIS is a verse of scripture which many people must
have found comforting, for it seems to reinforce our
most natural beliefs and prejudices, and attributes
them to God.

It satisfies our desire for a vague internationalism. 'He
created every race of men of one stock.' Our common
humanity. It was good Stoic doctrine, good Jewish doctrine,
all men being derived from Adam, and it is good Christian
doctrine, with Jesus Christ as the New Man, the first fruits of
God's new humanity. It can be translated into all sorts of
other terms, whether the brotherhood of man, or the self-
evident truth that all men are born equal. I remember some
years ago a fine exhibition of photographs called *The Family
of Man*. It was humanitarian rather than religious, and it
stressed that beneath all our differences is our common
humanity. We are one family.

But the text satisfies also our desire for nationalism. 'He
fixed the epochs of their history and the limits of their
territory.' Both our history and our geography are fixed by
the providence of God. We are people of a particular
tradition who belong in a particular place. There is a whole
range, a spectrum of beliefs and prejudices which might

seem to win support from such a text: ranging from our natural sense of belonging, our sense of home, our need to establish our identity in relation to a particular tradition, culture, place, to the nastier aspects of nationalism, the National Front in England, or, of course, Nazism in the Germany of the 1930s. In many parts of the world, in different languages, with different names inserted, you will find the same slogan chalked or spray-painted on walls: 'So & So, go home.' It may be 'Yankee, go home,' or 'Pakistani, go home,' or 'British, go home.' It says 'This is our territory; you don't belong here.' Not many of those who take such attitudes would bother overmuch about getting support from the Bible, but they might claim to find it here. 'He fixed the epochs of their history and the limits of their territory.' That is, each race has its own home, and should stick to it.

But if that were the case, of course, none of us has a right to be here. Though nations always like to pretend that the order they have established is the order given by God, few of us would be where we are if our ancestors had stuck in the beginning to some fixed place given them by God. The story of mankind is a story of the movement of peoples – and Paul or Luke (whichever of them is responsible for the form in which we have this discourse) must have known that. 'A wandering Aramean was my father,' said the Jew in his liturgy, and he saw the foundation of his nation in one who left his country and his kinsmen and his father's house, and went into the unknown, seeking another country.

And the story of that search is one of constant movement – Exodus, Exile and return. In fact the story of the Jews in the Old Testament is the story of mass immigration, aggression and conquest in which they are sometimes the aggressors and sometimes the victims; and while the Jewish settlement in Palestine may not have been so sweepingly successful as the Old Testament writers make it out to be, my sympathies are with the Amorites and the Canaanites and the Hittites and the Perizzites and the Hivites and the

Jebusites, who, as far as we can tell, were getting along quite happily and peacefully in the land flowing with milk and honey before the invasion of these religious fanatics who claimed that their God had given the land to them.

But who am I to complain? For I am possibly descended from some European invaders who settled in the south-east of Scotland, and pushed the original inhabitants away to the north and west. But were they the original inhabitants, or had they in their turn come from some breeding ground of migrant peoples in Central Asia? Perhaps others besides the Jews have to confess descent from a homeless wanderer. In South Africa even the Bantu are not the original inhabitants, having come down from the north to replace the disappearing Hottentot. Perhaps the correct model for mankind's story is not a static one, a map with fixed boundaries, but a dynamic one, the ceaseless movement of a river.

But if that were the case, then our text may be simply an example of religion performing a function it is always too willing to undertake – that of legitimising successful conquest or revolution. Such legitimising tends to happen anyway, with the passage of time and the realisation that you can't put the clock back. I recall a touching little piece of news I once noted. In 1976 nine Americans helped the British government to buy the estate of Battle in Sussex for the nation. They did it as a contribution to mark the American bicentennial, the two-hundredth Anniversary of the American Revolution. Now the estate of Battle, let me explain, contains the site of the Battle of Hastings, 1066, when William of Normandy defeated the English King and began the Norman Conquest of England. So our American friends commemorated a successful revolution against the English by enabling the English to commemorate a successful conquest over themselves. There is a gentle irony about that which appeals to me.

But as I say, my sympathies tend to be with the Perizzites,

or the Ancient Britons, or the Picts, or the American Indians, or the tribes of central Brazil. The suppressed peoples of the past and the oppressed peoples of today challenge the hypocrisy of our claim that it is God who has given us the land, and equally the hypocrisy of our sentiments about being all of a common stock, about the brotherhood of man, or those self-evident rights which belong to all men – except of course, Indians, Aborigines, and savages.

So I seemed to have talked myself quite out of sympathy with my text – a bad situation for a preacher.

So I look again at the passage, and I see that the religious commonplaces of verse 26 are set in the context of a call to man to leave his idols, and seek and find the true God – the God whose demand is repentance and whose promise is resurrection.

Let me try to see the internationalism and nationalism of our text in that context. I do it by taking two figures of our time – the Tourist, and the Exile.

The tourist and exile both leave their own countries and travel; both witness to the unity of mankind and to the diversity of nations – but they do it in different ways. You are tourists. You have come to St Andrews for three weeks of a Summer Institute. You hope to see a bit of Scotland, to learn a bit of Scots theology, maybe, and then go home again. You come because this place is different from home. Truly, it's not all that different – we speak different versions of the same language, though that in itself is a fruitful cause of misunderstanding; but if it were exactly the same as home, if we too had Howard Johnson on every motorway, it would hardly be worthwhile coming. The motive for tourism, it seems to me, is a good one; it is to enrich experience, to heighten awareness of the diversity of peoples, to cherish and respect that diversity, and to find, beneath it, the underlying unity of humanity.

But tourism today is open to two dangers. The first is that

it divides the world into those who can afford to be tourists and those who can't; those who visit and those who are visited. The second danger is that tourism itself tends to obliterate the real diversity of peoples, by making every tourist place look like every other tourist place. So you can travel the world without ever leaving America; you can go from the Chicago Hilton to the London Hilton, to the Nairobi Hilton . . . and so on, finding the same standard of comfort, the same standard of food – only the waiters having a different colour of skin.

I remember one visit to the cinema. The film we went to see was *All the President's Men*. I won't say anything of that (though it is relevant to our theme). Along with it was a British travelogue advertising a tour in the Caribbean. They began by showing us shots of a BOAC 747 taking off (from London I suppose) and then landing in Miami; and shots of the luxury liner that was to take the cruise. The script said that through modern transport exotic and romantic places are now within reach of everyone. Everyone? It didn't add 'everyone who can afford it'. The passengers on the ship were all white, though their chief preoccupation seemed to be to darken their skins as much as possible. The only black people one saw were working in the kitchens or trying to entertain. The liner floated among the islands of the Caribbean never touching at any point the poverty and the politics that are the realities of these islands. The corruption unconsciously exposed in that travelogue was a perfect balance to that uncovered in *All the President's Men*.

The tourist, whether a genuine explorer or a modern 'phony', has always a secure base at home. He knows who he is, if not always where he is. ('If it's Tuesday it must be Belgium', as one film put it.) The exile, on the other hand, leaves home not because he wants to, but because he must. For him there is no going back. He is bereaved. If the mark of modern tourism is cushioned comfort (even religious pilgrimages nowadays are advertised in terms of their comfort), the mark of the exile is suffering. The exile knows where he is; his problem is to establish exactly who he is, in relation to the home he has left, and the culture in which he is now set.

It has been my privilege to have Jewish friends who were refugees from Hitler's Germany in the 1930s. At the beginning of the war they were interned as enemy aliens, and it took our bumbling bureaucracy some time to tumble to the fact that these people were more loyal to the allied cause than most of the native population – because they had seen the horrors of Nazism; they knew what we were fighting against. But at the same time, because they didn't share many of our taken-for-granted assumptions about life, they saw some of the shortcomings of our society.

The exile seeks another country, a better country than the one he has perforce to leave. You can be an exile in spirit without leaving home. To be in exile in one's own country, because you can no longer share the taken-for-granted assumptions of your fellow citizens, but must stand in criticism, seeking a better country – this may demand more courage than physical exile. Dietrich Bonhoeffer is the example of the man who chose not to be in a literal sense the exile, the refugee, as he might have been, in Britain or America, but to return to Germany, to a different kind of exile in the midst of his own people.

The exile, I would suggest, rather than the tourist, is the model for the Christian in the world today. Perhaps if your tour makes you return a little more of an exile than before it will have done you good, The servant of the God who is always calling us away from our idolatries – of country, party, class, religion – is an exile. Precisely because he loves his home, but loves it in the light of another better country, a new humanity, he is a little bit of an alien within it. He stands uncomfortably pointing men to the God whose demand is repentance. But by that token, the exile is also the bearer to men of the promise of resurrection.

17 PEACE ON THE TRAIN

Readings: Job 26:6–14; I Corinthians 1:1–19; Luke 8:40–48

Text: I Corinthians 1:3 *Grace to you and peace from God our Father and the Lord Jesus Christ.*

SOME years ago I was on a visit to London for some meeting or other, which had finished early enough to let me catch the 4 o'clock King's Cross to Aberdeen train. I settled into my seat at King's Cross, and just before we were due to leave a friendly West Indian voice came over the PA system. 'This is your conductor speakin'. This is the 1600 hrs train from King's Cross to Aberdeen, calling at . . .' and he gave the list of stations, and I was reassured to hear Leuchars mentioned. (It's funny how you like that reassurance, even though you know perfectly well the train stops at Leuchars, and you wouldn't be there if it didn't.) Then in the customary way he went through the whole announcement again, but this time he ended 'Montrose, Stonehaven, Portlethen and Aberdeen. And may the peace of the Lord Jesus Christ be with you all.' There was a slight pause, then he continued, as if in embarrassment, 'If you will allow me. May God bless you all.' The effect was quietly sensational. Everyone looked at the passenger sitting opposite, whom up till that point, in true British fashion, we had been carefully ignoring. Eyebrows were raised, smiles broke out, and the general reaction was one of pleased surprise. The barriers between us were removed. It was an unusual experience to start a railway journey with a blessing. For me it was as if the flat matter-of-factness of our journeyings had been crossed by another dimension. Just for a moment we were reminded of the mystery of God's

102

presence and his peace in our lives.

I decided not to write and thank British Rail (as it then was) for this new service, in case the good man lost his job. I didn't know whether he made a habit of this, or, as I suspected, that he hadn't meant to do it, but being a minister or lay preacher in his own church he forgot for a moment where he was. But I had no doubt that it was completely sincere. He meant it.

The experience set me thinking. Why is it that, while I was delighted with the experience on the train (as we all were), I wouldn't want an order to go out to all train conductors 'You must end all announcements with a blessing.' It would then be a dreary routine. We feel, rightly, that there has to be a distinction between the duties of our daily work and the demands of our religion. Again, supposing that instead of ending with a nice warm blessing he had gone on, 'Stopping at . . . Stonehaven, Portlethen and Aberdeen, and the next stop for some of you will be Hell-fire if you don't repent and turn to the Lord.' I would have been the first to write and complain about this dreadful intrusion of our privacy.

So, one could ask a lot of questions about sacred and secular, about Church and State, on the basis of that experience. For the moment, I am simply intrigued by the fact that, perhaps because of the unexpected nature of the event, we found ourselves sitting in a train in King's Cross Station and being brushed by the mystery of things, touched by God's grace and peace.

It may be that we, more than previous generations, need to be reminded of this dimension of depth, this element of mystery in all our lives. Earlier generations have been more aware of our human limitations, and have stood in awe of that which they did not understand and could not control. Earthquake, thunder, wind and fire were all seen as pointers to the mysterious power and judgment of God. In the twenty-sixth chapter of Job we have a beautiful poetic recital of the wonders of God in nature, and then,

> Lo, these are but the outskirts of his ways,
> and how small a whisper do we hear of him!
> But the thunder of his power, who can understand?

The writer of Job understands how far the divine mystery eludes our grasp. He is in awe. Has our generation lost that sense of awe? With our scientific confidence and technological competence we may be less likely to see a divine mystery in or behind the elements of nature. (Oddly, I think that pioneering scientists often still have that sense of awe. It is those of us who have not gone down that road, but benefit from their discoveries, that have lost it.) Nor do we any longer look for God's majesty and mystery at the point where our knowledge ends and our ignorance begins: we wait for the next discovery to push back the frontiers of our ignorance. That at least is healthy. As Bonhoeffer taught us, God is not 'the God of the gaps'.

But dazzling and impressive as our scientific-technological world is (and I write this on a computer which I can't begin to understand), it can leave us with a two-dimensional picture of life. A surface existence, shallow living and shallow thinking. The world of the tabloids. If we are to see life solid, we need another dimension that crosses our scientific and material world, our commercial and political world, with the insights and values that give depth to life. What we need is not a separate sphere, where we turn our backs on this world to find another world of grace and peace. We need to be able to see this world, this material, commercial, scientific, technological, political world, in depth.

If you read the whole of the eighth chapter of Luke's Gospel, you will see that he is depicting an utterly hectic period in the life of Jesus – hectic and frustrating. Crowds thronging everywhere for his preaching and healing; his disciples slow on the uptake; his family being obstructionist.

When he tries to get away in a boat across the lake, there's a storm and they almost founder. On the other side there's a raving lunatic, and a people who are more annoyed about the loss of their pigs than overjoyed about the curing of the maniac. So back they go again, their holiday plans wrecked, and here are the crowds waiting, and an elder of the kirk with an urgent request for his dying daughter. Jesus decides to drop everything and go to her. Easier said than done: they can't make headway for the crowd. It must have been as bad as the World Cup, and far noisier than King's Cross Station.

And in that crowd, and wriggling her way through it is this puir wee body who's had a haemorrhage all these years. She shouldn't be there at all, for ritually she is unclean, but she's determined, and believes that, if she gets near enough to touch the outskirts of his ways, she will be cured. That's all she asks – to touch his coat. And she does it: she gets the touch.

'Who touched me?' The answer is 'Hundreds of people.' But that's not the point. Have you ever travelled on the London Underground in the rush hour? You are packed into these trains like herring in a barrel. Yet – have you noticed? – you don't touch anyone and nobody touches you. You are never so much alone as in an Underground train in the rush hour. If anyone were to touch me deliberately – anyone other than a pickpocket, that is – I would know. The Galilean crowd was, I'm sure, less restrained than the London one, but Jesus knew the touch of human need, quite different from any other touch. The frightened woman finds herself no longer clutching the hem of his garment, but looking up into eyes that reflect the sorrow and joys of the world. She hears a voice of infinite kindness say, 'Dear, you did it yourself. Your faith has healed you. Go in peace.'

In peace? In the middle of that struggling, bawling crowd? In peace, when he himself had been looking for peace for days and hadn't found any? Yes, in peace all right; peace and content, touched by his grace. The mystery of

God's grace and peace is in the midst of human life, not in retreat from it.

The woman touched Jesus in her need. I suppose many of our experiences of touching and being touched by the mystery of things are of that kind – boundary experiences, such as birth and death. It is an awesome experience when we see a new life come into the world, and sense the whole wonder of creation in the perfect, tiny fingernails of a new-born child. It is awesome in a different way when we watch one most dear leave this life, and we enter into the dark, baffling mystery of loss. Or, when, to our great surprise we touch him in the crisis of illness and the experience of suffering. The lines of Francis Thompson come to mind, as he echoes the Biblical stories and applies them to his London.

> But (when so sad thou canst not sadder)
> Cry – and upon thy so sore loss
> Shall shine the traffic of Jacob's Ladder
> Pitched betwixt Heaven and Charing Cross.
>
> Yea, in the night, my soul, my daughter,
> Cry – clinging heaven by the hems;
> And lo, Christ walking on the water
> Not of Gennesaret, but Thames.

But I would add two things. First, it is often through other people that we find ourselves touching Christ's garment, and being touched by his peace. I remember how once these same children (now grown-up), whose tiny fingernails I once admired, rallied round to parent their parents in a time of need, and touched us with the grace and peace of Christ.

Second, it is not only in times of crisis and of need. The bonus of God's blessing and his peace may come through some trivial incident, an unexpected kindness, a glimpse of beauty or a happy thought, through which our life is crossed as with a shaft of light. There is a saying, not in the Gospels, but attributed to Jesus: 'Lift the stone and you will find me, cleave the wood, and I am there.' Or, to quote Francis Thompson again, 'Turn but a stone and start a wing.'

The mystery of God's grace and peace is in the midst of human life, not somewhere away from it.

Perhaps that is what worship is for. Not to be the only place where we experience, each week, the mystery of God's grace and peace, but rather to be the place where our faith is renewed, where we are open again to the mystery, made more aware of the dimension that gives depth and solidity to all our life. So that then, in our daily living and all that it brings, we may be aware of the mystery that touches and surrounds our lives: to find Christ at our family tables as well as our communion tables, to see his love in the face of a friend, to hear his joy in the laughter of a child, to know his peace in the midst of the noise and the bustle and find his grace when we are most defeated.

And then, perhaps, we shall not be too surprised if he blesses us with his peace on the 1600 hrs train from King's Cross to Aberdeen.

18 HEALTH ABUNDANT

Service for the 50th anniversary of the National Health Service, St Mary's, Dundee, 5 July 1998

Readings: Isaiah 35; Luke 8:42b–48

Text: John 10:10b *I came that they may have life, and have it abundantly.*

THERE are two good reasons why we should today give God heartfelt thanks for the National Health Service. The first is, simply and obviously, the immense benefits the health service has brought to the people of this country during these 50 years. I suppose I was one of the first batch of part-time hospital chaplains to be appointed in the new health service in 1948, when I was a minister in Oban, and I have been a keen supporter of the health service since its beginning. Aneurin Bevan had to struggle against opposition from consultants and GPs, and had to overcome suspicion within his own party, but his vision was of a service that would bring the best of doctors and the best of medical care to everyone, free at the point of delivery. That vision has by and large been realised, though Bevan could not have foreseen the advance in medicine during these 50 years, enabling the service to do things he could not have imagined. The service he had to struggle to introduce is now the favourite institution of the British people. The nation loves the NHS, and is proud of it, and not without good reason.

The second reason why we should give God thanks today for the NHS is that it has survived all that has been done to it during these 50 years. No patient in the NHS has suffered so many unwanted treatments, so many untested and uncosted procedures (the internal market was never costed before it was introduced), so many prescriptions, surgical incisions, transplants and implants as the NHS itself. Many of us feared that this patient would die or be killed before its fiftieth birthday. But it is still alive, and still providing the best of care to all free at the point of delivery. Thanks to God, and thanks to you who are the National Health Service.

What of the future? I pray that the health service may have many years of health before it, free from unwanted interference, and that its own immune system may become strong enough to rid it of the diseases which have been allowed, or encouraged, to infect it in recent years.

I am appalled when I read that some doctors think that before the next 50 years are up the service will be financed by private health insurance. If that were to happen the NHS as we have known and loved it would be dead. The lucrative private health insurance industry in the USA and in this country is certainly bent on expansion, as its specious advertisements in our media show. But to yield to that pressure is to kill the health service. It is the American way, the most wasteful and unjust way. America has the most costly health care in the world, and it still leaves 37 million of its people without health cover, either because they are too poor or because they have chronic illnesses which lead the insurers to impose punitive premiums or to refuse to insure them altogether. A two-tier system contradicts the humanity, the vision which guided this service from the beginning. No road that way.

The convener of the Church and Nation Committee said recently, 'Health is a political matter.' She might have said, 'a political football'.

You may think I have been political enough already, but I hope you agree that a democratic government must continue to care for the health of its people, and that good health care, from the cradle to the grave, must never become a privilege which only the rich can buy. The rich will always want to buy privileges, else what's the point of being rich? Let them buy the frills, but not at the expense of the poor. It is a matter of political will. We spend less on health care than any other European country save Portugal, and too much of that is spent on a cumbersome management structure.

In the Old Testament, health is always seen as the blessing of God. But in an age when not much could be done about illness and human beings had simply to suffer the ills the flesh is heir to, the great vision of the prophets was of a time when there would be health for all. 'Then the eyes of the blind shall be opened, and the ears of the deaf unstopped; then shall the lame man leap like a hart, and the tongue of the dumb sing for joy.' That's a vision of health restored, of disablement and illness banished, of things as they should be.

It's a vision of a time that God alone can bring, and it is linked with a renewal of the earth. 'For waters shall break forth in the wilderness, and streams in the desert; the burning sand shall become a pool and the thirsty ground springs of water.' God's will for his children, his future, is health. But you cannot be healthy in an unhealthy environment. The earth must find its renewal too.

The vision is always beyond us. Total health in a good and fertile world. Yet it beckons us on, for it is the way things ought to be. In our modern technological society we have power that the ancient Israelites could not have dreamed of. We can remove cataracts and restore detached retinas, and make some of the blind see; we can give new hip joints and make some of the lame walk in comfort, if not literally leap for joy. That and so much else. The vision's there. Can we continue to plan with passion toward it?

In our modern technological society we have also the power to pollute the earth and the seas and the atmosphere. Our unbridled and reckless greed can turn the fertile land into the desert, and produce diseases and health problems that the Israelites never knew.

But it is also true that if we used our powers responsibly, if we curbed our greed, we could turn our man-made deserts into fertile fields again, and let pure water flow from our rivers to the seas, and in our cities breathe fresh air. And we could eat the foods that make us healthy, not those that destroy us. The vision's there. Can we reach towards it?

Perhaps that's what Alison Elliot meant when she said, 'Health is a political matter.' It is a matter of political will.

Turn now from the world of modern technology to the dusty roads and the crowded villages of first-century Galilee, where there walked this man, a remarkable teacher and preacher and healer. Jesus of Nazareth.

The Palestine of Jesus' day was different from that of the prophet Isaiah. It was more open to influences from Greece and Rome and from the East. The art of healing was practised, following the Hippocratic tradition, and Luke, the author of the Gospel, was himself a doctor. Alongside the professional doctors was what today we call 'alternative medicine' – healers who might conjure spirits, or pray or lay hands on the patient. Jesus was considered to be one of these, though he did not see himself as primarily a healer, but as a preacher and teacher, proclaiming the good news of God's love, announcing his Kingdom. When he healed it was a sign of the Kingdom, a foretaste of that vision.

Luke, being a doctor himself, shows considerable interest in the healing work of Jesus. The story we read, of the woman with the haemorrhage, Luke borrowed, as he did much else, from Mark. Like Mark he tells us that the woman had suffered this condition for 12 years, and that no one had been able to make her better. But Mark had said more. Mark said this: that the woman 'had suffered much under many physicians, and had spent all that she had, and was no better but rather grew worse' (Mk 5:26). Mark is telling the story from the patient's point of view, Luke from the doctor's. You could almost write the doctor's self-extenuating report for him. And also the patient's different experience. Today, she might not have spent all that she had, unless she lived in America, or was an old person in this country, with a chronic complaint, forced to live in a private nursing home. They do have to spend all that they have. We now have a health service from the cradle, but not, in all cases, to the grave.

I'm being political again. So back to our text. I am amused at the way Luke, in defence of his fellow doctors, alters Mark. It's the Medical Defence Union rallying round. Mark says the woman had suffered much at the hands of many doctors and had spent all that she had, and was no better but rather worse. Mark takes up the cudgels for this ill-treated woman. Luke cuts all that out and says only that no one had been able to heal her. He is loyal to his fellow professionals.

Here then is a chronic case of menorrhagia: at best an embarrassing and debilitating problem. In her society it made her ritually unclean, and she was debarred from worship and from much in normal life. Whether she had any business being in that crowd is an interesting question, but desperation gave her boldness. She squirmed and squeezed her way till she was in reach of the great man. She had no expectation of getting his attention. If she could touch the tassle of his robe.

She did, and it happened. Don't ask how, but she knew it happened. The bleeding stopped, and she was OK. She knew it. And he knew it too. 'Who touched me?' A stupid question in such a crowd. But some touches carry a message, of need, or of faith, or of love. Nurses know that, for the TLC (tender loving care) which good nursing gives is conveyed often in a touch. (Perhaps that was before they had to carry notebooks everywhere.) Anyway, the woman now has his full attention, though there is another patient waiting and the waiting list is growing. She finds him full of encouragement and grace.

And unlike those doctors who didn't cure her, he didn't ask a fee. Maybe here we have the remote beginnings of the National Health Service!

But more, much more than that. For Jesus is not primarily a healer, but one who calls us all, healthy and sick, out of death into life, out of fear into faith, out of a meaningless and boring existence into freedom to live and love and care. Out of living for ourselves to living for others. You could say that he calls us all to health. Yes, and even more. It's total well-being. It's life abundant. 'I came that they may have life, and have it abundantly.'

That is his promise. Nothing less can be our prayer today for those of you who work in the health service, for you cannot be the channels of healing for others if you yourselves feel undervalued, kicked around, and are full of anxiety, stress and needless pain, or if you're in it only for the money or the power. And that is our prayer for the patients and their families, which means all of us. Health is more than the containment or cure of this or that disease, the removal of this or that diseased organ. Health must open new possibilities of full and joyful living.

So may Jesus' promise come true for all of us. 'I came that they may have life, and have it abundantly.'

19 CURING OR COPING?

Readings: Isaiah 35; John 5:2–9

Text: John 5:6 *Do you want to be healed?*

ABOUT two years ago I cut out a small item from the paper. It was entitled 'Short Sighted', and this is what it said:

A group of good Samaritans in the Indian city of Delhi have had their offer of help soundly rejected at the People's Ideal School for the Blind. Medical volunteers examined the 30 residents and, finding that half could have their sight restored with a simple operation, offered to perform the procedure free of charge. But the school's blind director, J. S. Sharma, refused their offer and barred them from the building. Dr Dwardadas Motiwala, leader of the volunteers, is not surprised by the move. 'Schools such as this know that the support grants they receive will be cut if their enrolments are reduced.' Sharma remains unrepentant: 'My job is to teach the blind, not to treat their blindness.'

I was intrigued by this strange aspect of human nature. Here was someone, himself blind, who was dedicated to the education of the blind, in a country where blindness and poverty too often go together. Yet he was denying some of his pupils the priceless gift of sight.

I tucked the cutting away and had forgotten about it, until I read something in the news quite recently. This was about a new treatment for the deaf – an implant which could help some deaf people to hear and interpret speech. It would not

114

work with everyone, but it could help some to break out of the world of silence. And there was opposition to this from the quarter where you might least expect it: from the Association for the Deaf. They felt that deaf people were better within the deaf community, and should stay there. I'm giving you this as I remember it because unfortunately I didn't keep a cutting, but I hope I have the facts accurately.

The blind teacher who doesn't want some of his pupils to be given their sight. The Deaf Community which doesn't want some of its members to be given hearing. Is this another example of the old story – slaves who do not want their freedom, captives who come to love their chains?

Whatever we may make of miracles, we are presented in the New Testament with the picture of Jesus as a healer. He confronts people with an offer of wholeness, of health. 'Do you want to get well?' he asks the man at the pool at Bethzatha. The man replied that he had nobody to carry him to the pool and somebody always got there first. I've preached on this, I know, suggesting that it was just an excuse. He had been there 38 years, and had become used to his life as a cripple, and to his daily seat in the sun by the pool. How was it that in all these years he never got into the pool first? Maybe he didn't really want to. That's an interesting theory, but now I'm more inclined to see his answer as the literal truth. It's not easy for a lame man to win a race, unless he has swift and strong helpers.

In any case he accepts healing from Jesus, with apparent gratitude. And John is not interested in the psychological interchange between Jesus and the lame man. John is interested that there were others who objected to this healing. The Jews persecuted Jesus, because this had happened on the Sabbath. So all our examples so far are of people finding reasons why other people shouldn't be made whole, healthy, fully functioning. The blind teacher in India, the Deaf Association in this country, the religious people in first-century Jerusalem.

But notice that Jesus didn't heal everyone who was sick in Palestine. John says there was a multitude of invalids, blind, lame, paralysed, lying at the pool of Bethzatha. One only saw Jesus looking at him and saying, 'Do you want to get well?' Mark tells how at the start of his ministry in Capernaum Jesus healed many sick, and, as the news of this spread, they kept bringing more, and the disciples wanted to stay and enjoy this, but Jesus moved on, saying, 'I have to preach in other towns too.' Jesus didn't feel he had a mission to eliminate all disease. He didn't go looking for people to heal. Yet he never regarded disease or disability as a good thing: he held before people a vision of health, of wholeness in body and spirit.

Now I can give another, very different example. I have just been reading a remarkable book called *The Diving-Bell & the Butterfly*. It is by Jean-Dominique Bauby, and is a translation from the French. In December 1995, this man, aged 42, editor-in-chief of *Elle* magazine, suffered a massive stroke which left him unable to speak and able to move only his left eyelid. Yet mentally he was clearly unimpaired. The book is a series of reflections on his condition and on his previous life, and it was dictated, letter by letter, using an alphabet board which allowed his helper to read out the letters until he winked at the right one. An astonishing feat and a touching book. His courage in seeking to reach out from his diving-bell helped others, and led to the formation of an Association for the Locked-in Syndrome as it is called. For him release from the diving-bell came by death. But for others, the struggle goes on.

What comes out of all this?

First, I believe there is a call to heal whenever healing is possible. Modern medicine can do what in a previous age would have been a miracle. Cataracts can be removed, detached retinas repaired. Heart by-pass surgery and the humble pacemaker can make people well, some who might otherwise die. Perhaps in time genetic research may show

how we can stop cancer developing, and offer us gentle and not violent treatment for cancer. And, of course, better diet and better lifestyles might help more people to live fuller and longer lives. We go on hoping.

But meantime there are many for whom healing waters do not flow. There are still innumerable conditions for which modern medicine cannot do more than make life more tolerable and comfortable. And this is the second point: one of the great advances in our time has been in helping the disabled to live as full and as enjoyable a life as their condition will allow – often far more full and far more enjoyable than they or their grandparents could have imagined.

We look for wheelchair access to public buildings. The General Assembly now provides interpreters for the deaf. The most moving experience I had in India was to visit the hospital at Kanchipurum, where we in Hope Park had given money for a well, in memory of Dr Douglas. But it wasn't the well that moved me most. It was the sight of young people wearing calipers and hopping around on crutches. A livelier and happier bunch I never saw. They were victims of a polio epidemic. The hospital had discovered them in the villages, sitting in the corners of huts, and had brought them in, cut their shrunk tendons, given them calipers and elbow crutches, and was teaching them trades. This was life, life from a living death, given in the name of Christ. The sight of a young girl dancing beautifully from the waist up, because her legs were useless, touched my heart. And the hospital had done something more: they had embarked on a programme of inoculation, in the hope that polio could be eliminated.

The hospital had it right. They were helping these young people to live full and useful lives in spite of their disabilities, and they were doing all they could to ensure that no one else should suffer such disability.

Our age specialises in coping with disability. (Incidentally,

I don't find anything of this attitude in the Bible, other than perhaps Paul's response to his thorn in the flesh.) We rightly admire the clubs and associations for the handicapped, and the grit of people who take part in paraplegic games, and so on. Good is coming out of evil. A Christian thing, surely, in which we must rejoice.

But that doesn't make the impairment or disability a good thing. And what if you come to regard your impairment as a distinction, your handicap a superiority? What if the community of the disabled becomes so attractive that you would not ask to leave it? It seems to me that is happening with some of the impaired groups in our society, and accounts for some of the bizarre things that go on. Some impairments ask not to be regarded as impairments any more, but as 'alternative life-styles'. I'm sure you can think of examples.

You have perhaps heard the new answer to the question 'How many social workers does it take to change a light bulb?' The answer is 'None: they sit round and form a group on "Coping with Darkness".' There are times when there is no alternative but to cope as best we can with the darkness, and there can be triumph in that. But it is better to find a light bulb and have light again.

We are all impaired in some way, in body and in spirit. And we have to beware lest we come to love our impairment, for the excuse it gives us whenever things go wrong or get tough. It was once suggested that when you can't remember someone's name you should ask after their old complaint, and they will talk about their illness or their back pains long enough to give you a clue as to who it is you're talking to.

We have to live with ourselves and with each other the way we are. There is a lot we just have to put up with, as best we can. But we mustn't love our crutches, if there is a chance of throwing them away.

The woman with the issue of blood believed that if she could only touch Jesus' robe she would be rid of the haemorrhage and whatever was causing it – and she was. The blind man crying by the roadside heard a voice asking, 'What do you want?' and he didn't say, 'A guide dog', he said, 'Lord, that I may see again', and he did.

Don't mistake me. Guide dogs are great; wheelchairs are wonderful; so are calipers and elbow crutches and spectacles and hearing aids and pacemakers. But Isaiah's vision of the day of God is better:

Then the eyes of the blind shall be opened,
And the ears of the deaf unstopped;
Then shall the lame man leap like a hart,
And the tongue of the dumb sing for joy.
Would you like to get well?

Now unto him who by the power at work within us is able to do far more abundantly than all that we ask or think, to him be glory in the church and in Christ Jesus, to all generations, for ever and ever. Amen.

20 THE REIGN OF CHRIST THE KING

Readings: Jeremiah 23:1–6; Luke 23:33–43

Text: Luke 23:42 *And he said, 'Jesus, remember me when you come in your Kingly power.'*

WHEN I can't decide what passage I ought to preach from on any Sunday I reach for the lectionary in Common Order. I found that the Sunday between 20 and 26 November is headed 'Reign of Christ the King'. This is a new one on me. I never knew of such a feast. Every Sunday in our prayers or hymns or in the Creed we confess Christ as King, as the early church did when it asserted, 'Jesus is Lord'. But if 'The Reign of Christ the King' is the theme for today, then so let it be, and the lessons as given.

Luke tells of two terrorists who were crucified alongside Jesus. The word is literally 'evildoers', so could mean 'criminals' or 'thieves' or 'robbers'. I'm sure they were rebels, resistance fighters whom we would call terrorists. The Jews hated Roman rule, and some fanatics believed that armed rebellion could topple the power of Rome. Crazy, but the people had more sympathy with them than with time-serving quislings who kept their lucrative jobs by collaborating with the occupying power.

But terrorists get caught and three had been. The only one whose name we know was their leader. Barabbas was popular with the mob. They had been easily persuaded to ask Pilate for his release instead of Jesus. So Jesus took the central place, the place of the leader, between the two members of the gang.

An ill-assorted group. Jesus had harmed no one. He was

there because he challenged the heart of Jewish religion and threatened the power of the priests, because he taught God's free forgiveness, because he showed them the way of love.

Yet there are hints in the gospels that he had contacts with the movement for armed rebellion, and that they had tried to recruit him as their leader. They had in common a passionate love for their people. But for the Zealots the end of Roman rule was all that mattered. Jesus saw that God's Kingdom required a deeper transformation in people's thought and life. Yet he was well known to the terrorists, for his preaching and healing. Many hoped that he was the coming Christ, the Son of God, who would establish God's Kingdom.

But he hangs on a cross, between two violent men. No kingdom for him now, it seems. And Luke records the strangest conversation between the three men hanging there in agony. The first turns all his anger on to Jesus, taking up the mocking of the mob. He railed, Luke says. 'Are you not the Christ? Save yourself and us.' What kind of a miracle-worker was this, who couldn't perform a miracle to save his own life?

He spits at Jesus his anger and his agony. And Jesus has nothing to say. But the answer comes from the other side. 'Have you no fear of God? We are justly condemned. But this man has done nothing wrong.' Then to Jesus he says, 'Jesus remember me when you come in your kingdom.'

What a strange thing for a man on a cross to say to one crucified by his side. Was it a sad and gentle irony? Or did he see what no one else there saw, that even on a cross this man was a king?

The answer is even more surprising. 'Truly, I say to you, today you will be with me in Paradise.' He is talking to a rebel, possibly a murderer. Both are about to die the most cruel and painful death imaginable. But the word is the word of supreme confidence, authority, and a gracious promise. 'Truly, I say to you, today you will be with me in Paradise.'

The word 'truly' is the Hebrew word AMEN, which we use rather feebly at the end of our prayers. On Jesus' lips it is always a momentous word of emphasis and authority. This is the word of a king, and it is full of grace, and it says 'today': not sometime or at the end of time. Even on the cross, his Kingdom is at hand.

Now, back to what we read from Jeremiah. Jeremiah longed to see God's Kingdom, but what he saw in his native Judah was not encouraging. Already the Northern Kingdom of Israel had been conquered, and its people scattered. Things are going the same way in Judah. Jeremiah blames the government, as most of us do when things go wrong. The shepherds in Jeremiah, as in Ezekiel, are the rulers. They should be ruling under God, but instead rule for their own benefit. Careless and corrupt government, government that cares more for money than for people, has left the people to suffer. That's Jeremiah's complaint. And he looks forward to the day when there will be a king who is wise and just and sets things right.

Most of us share Jeremiah's disappointment that the world is not better governed. Perhaps I should watch what I say here, for I complained openly about the mud-slinging and scaremongering that passes for political debate just now, and I blamed the government for it. That's what governments are for! Someone once said, 'Governments are like wheelbarrows – useful implements, but they need to be pushed!' So we push them to do better. I don't mind that, though they also deserve credit when they're doing quite well. But neither Donald Dewar nor Tony Blair would pretend that what we have in Scotland now is the Kingdom of God. The kingdoms of this world are still far from the Kingdom of God.

So what is the Reign of Christ the King which we are to celebrate today? Is it at the end of time? Perhaps, but the dying Jesus doesn't say to the dying terrorist, 'At the end of the world, you'll see.' He speaks like a king already, and says,

'Today'. His Kingdom is a spiritual kingdom. It is here, at hand, as he was so fond of saying.

Is the church then the Kingdom of God? The Catholic Church has claimed this, and perhaps still does. But when the church has sought to rule the world it has been the most intolerant, cruel, persecuting, oppressive tyranny. The organised church is certainly not the Kingdom, and when it claims to be it becomes demonic.

How then does Christ reign in the world today? Look at the man on the cross. He is the man for others, and his way of truth and love and sacrifice is the way of the Kingdom. Spiritual, not political.

But that does not mean that Christ's reign has nothing to do with the world or the way it is governed. His way of truth and love stands in judgment over all our attempts to live together here on earth. And when we deny his reign, turn our backs on the things Jesus stands for, we end in chaos and misery.

That is why democracy is important. Reinhold Niebuhr once said, 'Man's capacity for justice makes democracy possible; man's capacity for injustice makes democracy necessary.' Because we can cooperate to seek a better, juster society, democracy is possible. Because we tend to get things wrong, to see things from one selfish point of view, we need the checks and balances of democracy. No party has all the truth, no party has all the virtues. We need to remember that.

That is why Christians can be found in all political parties, and why it is sad when politicians or parties lose respect for each other. If ever I drive over to Earlsferry I like to stop before the Town Hall there. There is a plaque in honour of the golfer, James Braid. It says, 'He had many opponents, but no enemies.' That is a tribute to the spirit in which he played the game and the fact that he never turned his opponents into enemies. I wish our politicians could learn that.

The reign of Christ the King stands in judgment over human government, whether in church or in state, and calls us to bring the things of earth a little closer to the things of heaven. We do that best when we respect one another, listen to one another, for none of us has a monopoly of wisdom, justice or love.

We can see signs of his reign and be glad. We are the heirs of the Christian centuries. Our society has been stained, imperfectly indeed, but indelibly, by the Christian faith and by Christian conscience. Long struggles of reform have not been in vain. That is why we are not lamenting a morass of corruption, rulers that care for nothing but lining their own pockets. In some countries still that is the way of life. In ours, when it happens, it draws universal condemnation. We have reason to be grateful for Christ's reign among us.

Our New Testament story told us that the Reign of Christ the King is the Reign of Christ the Crucified. Proclaiming the reign of Christ is not always a rosy path. Men have died a painful death for it, and we in St Andrews have the memorials of the martyrs, on the Scores and on the cobbles outside the Chapel, the Castle and Dean's Court. Today people don't suffer so dramatically, but many a man or woman of principle has been told, 'If you take this stand now, you need never expect promotion, you need never hope to hold Cabinet office.' Some have yielded to the blackmail, but others have made the sacrifice, because they cared more for others than for themselves.

In such people Christ reigns, and in his reign we may rejoice.

21 OUT OF DARKNESS INTO LIGHT

Memorial Service for the 16 children and their teacher who were killed in Dunblane Primary School on 13 March 1996. Held in Dunblane Cathedral, 9 October 1996.

Readings: Isaiah 60:1–3, 19–72; I John 1:5–9; Revelation 22:1–5

Text: John 8:12 *When Jesus spoke again to the people, he said, 'I am the light of the world. Whoever follows me will not walk in darkness, but will have the light of life.'*

WHEN this Memorial Service was being planned a theme emerged: the theme 'Out of darkness into light'. About the darkness no one had any doubt. Darkness fell on many families and indeed on this entire community on the morning of 13 March. Light was turned into darkness. Yet in a Memorial Service, even after only six months – and six months is a short time in the history of grief – darkness cannot be allowed the last word. 'The light shines in the darkness, and the darkness has not overcome it,' says St John. The last word must still be with light.

Out of darkness into light. For many of you that must still be an expression of faith, not of feeling. In such a time no one should be asked to pretend to feelings that they do not, or don't yet, have. To be honest, with ourselves, and with each other, and before God, is the first requirement of our healing. Grief is a minefield of emotion. Our feelings come and go. Yet even in the darkest night, we may, we must, believe in the light, look for and long for the light.

Our act of Remembrance today used the symbolism of light. It seems so natural and appropriate. By lighting the candles and by reading the names you, as a community, have remembered before God each individual who died in the massacre on 13 March.

Each of these candles represents a unique human life.

The candle is a good symbol, especially for the children. It is small, yet it is a bright, warm light. My wife used to teach Primary I, and she wouldn't have exchanged that for any other job in the world, because of her delight in these children, their openness, their eagerness to learn and the brightness they brought into the classroom. So would it be, I'm sure, with Gwen. The Primary I teacher is like a mum to her children.

But the candle is also a symbol of fragility, vulnerability. It is easily snuffed out. Such is our life, and the life of the child.

Each candle today is a life that we remember, a light that God gave to us, even if for only a little while. When someone dies young, as these did, we tend to think of what they might have been, of what they were becoming. A young woman with so much of her life still before her. Young children at a most delightful stage of their development.

Children change so quickly, as our photograph albums remind us. These will change no more. Yet we value them for what they were, not for what they might have been. They gave us light for a little time, and we remember that light with thankfulness.

I often think of friends of mine, from school and university, who were killed in the war. In their early 20s, most of them. Here am I, an old man now. But what of them, my classmates and contemporaries?

They shall grow not old, as we that are left grow old.
Age shall not weary them, nor the years condemn.

Laurence Binyon's words seem less a lament than a blessing. As we remember those who died on 13 March, we need not think too much of what they might have been. We value what they were. Jesus valued children, not for what they might become, but for what they already were. He set a child in the midst of the disciples, not so that they could teach the child something, but so that the child should teach them a lesson: a lesson about God's Kingdom. Children, for Jesus, were examples of the Kingdom of God, and of how to receive it. They have a quality, of acceptance, of hope, of trust, that we need to retain, no matter how long we live, and no matter what happens to us. To accept God's forgiveness, like a child, to trust his goodness, like a child, means keeping alive the child in us. Perhaps remembering these bright lights, as we do today and will in years to come, may help keep in us the child-like heart, the open, trusting, hopeful heart, the spirit of God's Kingdom.

Apart from that, I have a strange feeling that age doesn't matter very much in heaven, where all lives are fulfilled. Perhaps in God's Kingdom we are all the ages we ever were, or might have been. When I meet my friends there, we shall still be contemporaries. When you at last meet your children, they may be wiser and more serene than you could have imagined. So don't let us sentimentalise them. They also must move on into yet more light.

Thou hast come safe to port, I still at sea.
The light is on thy head. Darkness in me.

I once found these words strangely comforting. The thought that light was on her head helped me in my darkness. The light is on their heads. Even when we still grope in darkness, the glory of the Lord is risen upon them. That contains the promise that for us, too, light will come.

'I am the light of the world,' said Jesus. 'Whoever follows me will not walk in darkness, but will have the light of life.' The text, like our theme, 'out of darkness into light', implies that we all must make a journey. Those who lost a dear one, clearly. The survivors, who lost their innocence that dreadful morning, whose lives are scarred, have their journey to make. And all of us who share the horror, must make our journey out of that horror into a safer, more civilised society.

I said earlier that each candle represents a unique human life. They were different from one another, these bright little buttons. So are we all different from one another, and no one, minister or counsellor, can dictate the route we must follow in our particular journey from darkness into light. Even in one family we may take different routes, and that can require much understanding and tolerance and concern for each other within the family. I cannot tell you how the light will return. One thing I know. As long as we stand still, none of us will find it. *Solvitur ambulando*. It will become clear as we walk. As we follow him who is the world's true light, we begin to discern the light.

So we dare not get stuck. When things like this happen, you find yourself cast in a new role – bereaved parent, bereaved family, whatever. It is unbearably painful, but it also confers on you a certain kind of distinction, importance, a new identity. You are a victim. Now that is true. That is the dreadful experience you must come to terms with. But for your children's and the other children's sakes, you cannot let what happened to you become your whole identity. We must never give the other children the impression that to be valued, a child must be dead. That is to close the door against life, against the future. You are never just a victim. You are who you are, and what you do. The door must open to beckon you, not to forget, never to forget, but to take your experience into the future, though it is a different future from the one you yourself had planned.

I don't think any of us will ever have a completely satisfying explanation of why such terrible things happen in this world, why they happen to us, why they happen to innocent children. Christianity does not offer us an intellectual explanation. It offers us the story of a man on a cross, God's own son sharing our suffering, sharing our darkness, until in him we find the light. He is the victim who became the victor, and gives us the victory too.

Out of darkness into light. 'Whoever follows me,' said, Jesus, 'will not walk in darkness, but will have the light of life.'

I said we must each find our own way, our own route, out of darkness into light. Perhaps I should rather have said, 'God has his own way with each of us.' Our ways will be different, but they will, I suspect, have this in common. As we follow him who is the world's true light, we begin to see bits of the jangled, jagged nonsense of our lives falling into place, making some kind of pattern. No loss is a dead loss. In all loss there is gain. The mistakes we have made, the suffering we so regret having caused to others, become occasions to learn and to know more deeply God's forgiveness and his grace. The awful things that have happened, to us, to our children or our friends, may become occasions to know more deeply the infinite value of human love, the strength of human sympathy, and to know, perhaps for the first time, the mystery of the divine love and the serenity that finally banishes resentment and bitterness, and leads us into peace.

May the light of the world go with each of us in our journeyings through life. For he has promised, 'Whoever follows me will not walk in darkness, but will have the light of life.'